THE OPEN UNIVERSITY

UNDERSTANDING SOCIETY: A FOUNDATION COURSE   UNITS 32–36

The Population Explosion — an Interdisciplinary Approach

THE OPEN UNIVERSITY PRESS

The Open University Press
Walton Hall Bletchley Bucks

First published 1971. Reprinted 1972, 1973
Copyright © 1971 The Open University

All rights reserved
No part of this work may be
reproduced in any form, by
mimeograph or any other means,
without permission in writing
from the publishers

Designed by the Media Development Group of the Open University

Printed in Great Britain by
EYRE AND SPOTTISWOODE LIMITED
AT GROSVENOR PRESS PORTSMOUTH

SBN 0335 01508 5

Open University courses provide a method of study for independent learners through an integrated teaching system, including textual material, radio and television programmes and short residential courses. This text is one of a series that makes up the correspondence element of the Social Sciences Foundation Course.

For general availability of supporting material referred to in this text, please write to the Director of Marketing, The Open University, Walton Hall, Bletchley, Buckinghamshire.

Further information on Open University courses may be obtained from the Admissions Office, The Open University, P.O. Box 48, Bletchley, Buckinghamshire.

CONTENTS

UNIT 32   **THE DEMOGRAPHER AND HIS WORLD**
Michael Drake   Page 9

33   **DEMOGRAPHIC REGIONS OF THE INDIAN SUBCONTINENT**
Andrew Learmonth   Page 29

34   **POPULATION AND ECONOMIC GROWTH**
Leslie Wagner   Page 69

35   **POPULATION GROWTH AND SOCIAL AND POLITICAL SYSTEMS**
Ruth Finnegan and David J. Murray   Page 97

36   **DIFFUSION AND ACCEPTANCE OF CHANGE**
Hedy Brown   Page 139

INTRODUCTION TO UNITS 32—36

The population of the world is now approximately 3,700 millions. It is currently increasing by between seventy and eighty millions a year: a rate of increase which, if continued, would lead to a population of almost 7,000 millions by the year 2000. Increase at this rapid rate is a relatively recent phenomenon in the history of the world (see back cover) and this is partly why we talk of the 'population explosion'. But we also use the term because population growth of this magnitude, especially since it is concentrated in the less economically developed parts of the world, is regarded as a potentially destructive force. The growth and decline of populations has long been recognised as having far reaching effects on political, social and economic systems as well as on man's spatial arrangements and maybe even on the individual psyche. It is not surprising, therefore, that the currently unprecedented rate of population growth should be seen as having correspondingly unprecedented effects. (That some of the supposed effects are, however, if not unfounded, then at least unproven, is demonstrated in Unit 35.)

The scale and magnitude of the phenomenon that has come to be called the 'population explosion' is then one reason why we chose to end this Foundation Course, by focussing upon it the attention of all the disciplines that have contributed to the course. There were, however, a couple of other reasons and although neither emerges as clearly as one might have hoped, it is perhaps worthwhile noting them.

First, we wanted to end the course, as it had begun, by demonstrating how an interdisciplinary analysis of a social phenomenon can heighten our understanding of it. In the first units we directed attention at what one might term an 'academic question' (Why do people live in societies?) using that term in its everyday, rather pejorative sense. In ending, however, we wanted to demonstrate that the social scientist, though an academic, has another facet to his character, namely a sensitivity to matters of immediate public concern. Such matters often arouse intense emotions and value-laden judgements. It is a task of the social scientist to analyse them as objectively as possible, even though in choosing to study them at all he reveals the subjective side of his nature.

Secondly, this being the final section of the course, we wanted to recall some of the other matters we have discussed during the past year. Naturally we did not want to do this in an arid, repetitive revision session and so we chose a topic which would in itself generate what one might call – if you'll forgive the expression – 'backward linkages'. Population studies do that for they embrace so much. To give but one example of this, Zelinsky (1966), p. 53, remarks 'There is no escaping the thesis that the pursuit of any significant question in population geography inevitably familiarises the student with every aspect of geography and many of its neighboring fields'. In working through Units 32–36, you should, therefore, bear in mind the insights provided by earlier units and through a process of cross fertilisation seek to add to your understanding of the course as a whole. Here are some pointers to this end.

Unit 32 seeks to demonstrate the importance, when examining

any social phenomenon, of being precisely sure of what one is examining, of precisely what one's data does and does not show. This truth is illustrated by an examination of the way a demographer seeks to measure population change. The precise definition of concepts and the importance of quantitative analysis has, of course, been remarked upon many times throughout the course.

Unit 33 seeks to further illustrate the importance of clarity of definition by indicating how a geographer relates the phenomenon under discussion to the spatial context in which it takes place. Thus although superficially the population experience of India may appear homogeneous, and in many contexts is treated as such, in fact the geographer by a precise mapping of that experience is able to demonstrate and clarify important regional variations, which could well have important policy implications. As already mentioned the example taken here is India, the problems of which are referred to on a number of occasions throughout this section of the course, in an attempt to provide another point of focus.

In Unit 34 the relationship between population growth and economic development is discussed – with especial reference to underdeveloped economies. Population problems in this context, as in several others, lend themselves to analysis at the micro (the family) and the macro (the community) level and, therefore, pose interesting parallels with the presentation of economic theory in earlier units. Unlike earlier economic units, however, Unit 34 goes much further in seeking to apply economic concepts to actual situations, so complementing and, hopefully, validating, as it were, the earlier preoccupation with abstractions.

Unit 35 has already been mentioned. Apart from questioning the conventional wisdom – the goal of all social scientists and a prime aim of this course – this unit recalls a number of the themes dealt with in earlier units, especially by the sociologists. These include the function of the family, the interrelatedness of all human experience and its enormous variety, the 'difficulty of disentangling single causes from the complex web of society' and the social as opposed to the biological bases of behaviour.

The final unit of the section (Unit 36) examines from the sociopsychological point of view, the problems involved in getting people to accept an innovation. There are many echoes here of earlier units on socialisation, on attitudes, on group behaviour. The case study which ends the unit is of a family planning programme; the context is India: the problem is one affecting the second most biologically based of all man's needs and so takes us back to the opening unit of the course.

It is hoped that by the end of this section of the course you will agree with us – at least in part – first, that to examine the society around us as a social scientist does, provides new insights and enhances understanding, and second, that to focus a number of the social sciences on a particular aspect of social life, deepens that understanding. This course as a whole has been an exercise in what I like to think of as 'social science literacy'. Just as to be literate in the conventional sense causes one to restructure the world, so to be 'social science literate' brings yet another perspective to bear. Of course it would be pretentious of us to suggest that we have done very much or done it very well. But if you feel that we have at least laid the foundations of 'social science literacy', got across the ABCs as it were, we shall be satisfied and we hope that you will.

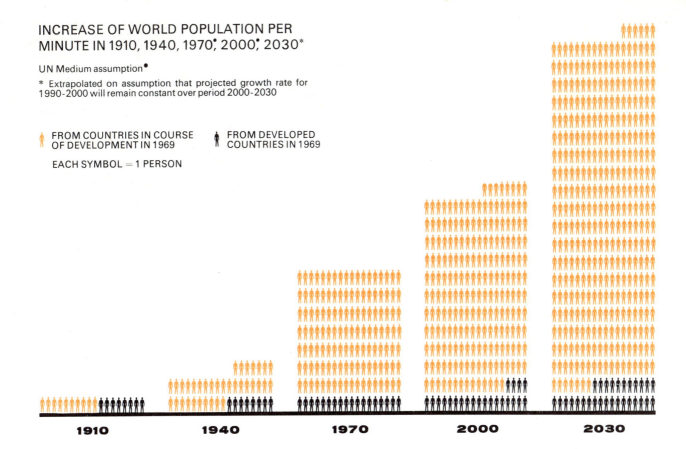

SUPPLEMENTARY MATERIALS (bound separately, and at present available only to Open University Students).

Self-assessment tests
Computer marked assignments
Radio notes
Television notes
Notes on the correspondence material

THE SET BOOKS

Understanding Society.* Readings in the Social Sciences edited by The Social Sciences Foundation Course Team. London, Macmillan (1970).

Society by E. Chinoy. New York, Random House (1967).

Prologue to Population Geography by W. Zelinsky. New Jersey, Englewood Cliffs (1966).

* Referred to in the text as the *Reader*.

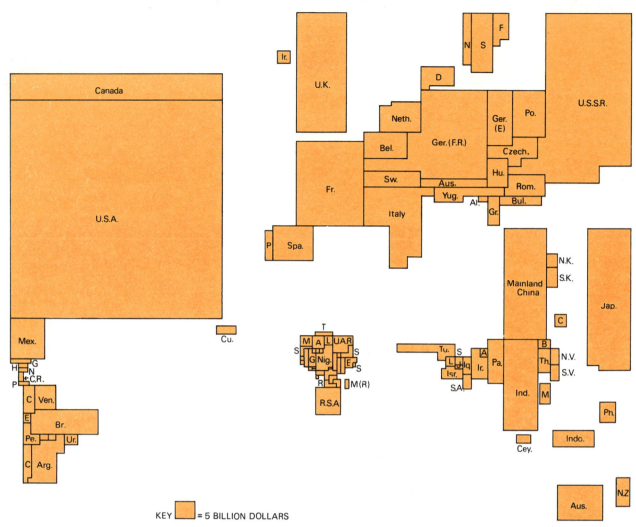

Gross National Product (G.N.P.) by Country, 1968 (Billions of U.S. dollars of 1964).

Unit 32
The Demographer and his World

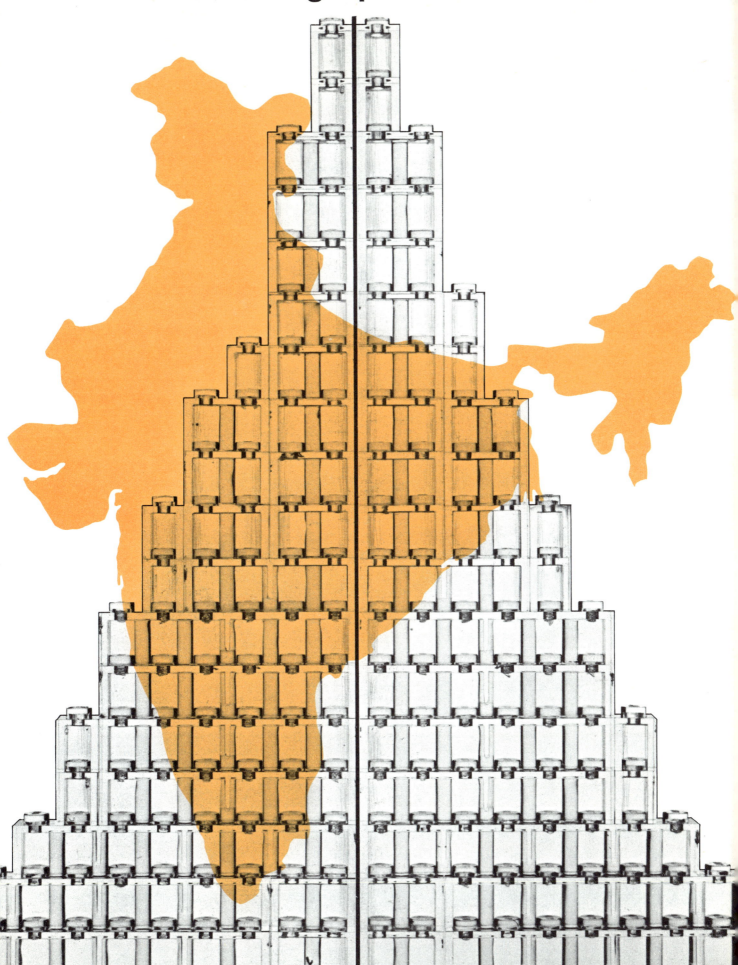

CONTENTS UNIT 32

		PAGE
1	INTRODUCTION	13
2	WHAT DO WE MEAN BY POPULATION?	13
3	THE MEASUREMENT OF POPULATIONS	15
	3.1 The Census	15
	3.2 Vital Registration	15
4	THE STRUCTURE OF POPULATION	16
	4.1 The Sex Ratio	16
	4.2 The Population Pyramid	16
5	POPULATION CHANGE	18
	5.1 The Crude Birth Rate	18
	5.2 The Crude Death Rate	18
	5.3 The Standardised Mortality Rate	20
	5.4 The General Fertility Rate	20
	5.5 The Child-Woman Ratio	21
	5.6 The Total Fertility Rate	22
	5.7 Gross and Net Reproduction Rates	23
	5.8 The Application of Demographic Tools	24
6	THE VERIFICATION OF DEMOGRAPHIC DATA	24
	6.1 The Politics of Demographic Data	24
	6.2 The Psychology of Age Reporting	25
	6.3 The Geography of Population Distribution	26
	6.4 The Economics of Family Formation	26
	6.5 The Sociology of Co-operation	27
7	CONCLUSION	27
	ACKNOWLEDGEMENTS	28
	BIBLIOGRAPHY	28

THE DEMOGRAPHER AND HIS WORLD

1 INTRODUCTION

The demographer can be described as that member of the social science fraternity whose primary concern is with the statistical study of human populations. Why then introduce him at this late stage in the course? There are several reasons. First, his is the discipline whose interests are most central to the so-called 'population explosion': the phenomenon we shall be considering over the next five weeks. Second, his is a social science that is especially dependent upon *numeracy* and the *precise definition of concepts*. Both are, of course, present in all the social sciences and both have appeared throughout this course, but in demography they are of paramount importance, because the discussion of population problems is virtually meaningless without the use of quantitative data set in a tight conceptual framework. In other words, the demographer needs to be sure of precisely what he is measuring and of how to go about it. Examining the work of the demographer in both these regards is then a convenient reminder that, by this stage in the course, you should be making sure, in your own mind, of the key concepts and measures that have been discussed in earlier units.

TEST 1

The third reason for introducing the demographer at this point in the course is that his work demonstrates, perhaps more clearly than any other social scientist, the need for interdisciplinary collaboration. For, as we shall see, because he is so dependent upon quantitative data, he needs to be sure of precisely what that data does, or does not, show. In this crucial task of verifying his numbers he must needs draw frequently upon the insights – sometimes of a substantive nature, sometimes of a methodological one – of his colleagues in sociology, economics, political science, geography and psychology, to mention only the disciplines represented in this course.

Over the next few pages I shall, therefore, discuss some of the concepts and some of the measures used by the demographer, as well as some of the interests of his social science colleagues that are of a particular concern to him.

2 WHAT DO WE MEAN BY POPULATION?

In everyday language we conceive of a population in rather static terms. If we ask the question – 'What is the population of Bletchley?' we might expect to hear some such reply as 'about 23,000'. If we ask – 'What is the population of England and Wales?' we would expect a figure of 'about 47,000,000'. In fact, of course, a moment's reflection is sufficient to make us realise that, when we say the population of Bletchley is 23,000 or that of England and Wales is 47,000,000, we mean that at a particular point in time, usually when a census or count was taken, the population was of such a magnitude. But why do we not expect to hear a precise figure?

After all, at the census taken in 1966, the number of people counted in Bletchley was 23,140; in England and Wales it was 47,136,451. We don't expect to hear such a figure, I suggest, partly because it would be difficult to remember but far more importantly because, as everyone realises, populations are constantly changing as time passes; births and immigration causing them to increase and deaths and emigration causing them to decrease. A population then might be defined as *a flow of persons through time*. At first, such a definition may be a little difficult to grasp and certainly its implications are one of the main hazards of population studies. A pictorial analogy might help.

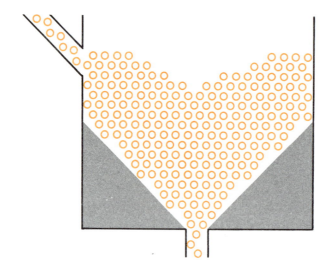

Figure 32.1

Imagine a box full of marbles. It has a hole near the top and an outlet at the bottom. Marbles are fed into the box at a certain rate and are released from it at a certain rate. At any particular time the number of marbles in the box will depend upon the size of these two rates and the length of time they have been maintained. Let us suppose that they are exactly equal at the present time: thirty marbles per minute coming in, thirty marbles per minute going out. Then the number of marbles in the box will remain the same. But the composition of the body – or population – of marbles will be changing constantly. For every minute thirty *new* marbles are coming in and thirty *old* marbles are going out. The analogy with human populations is pretty obvious. If we think of the marbles coming in as births and those going out as deaths and the marbles in the tank as a human population, one can see where we get our definition of a population as *a flow of persons through time*. A population is, therefore, a dynamic not a static phenomenon and it is this particular characteristic of human populations that poses special problems for the demographer trying to measure population change and even more so when he tries to predict its future behaviour. Because populations are changing constantly and because their structure affects the processes by which they change and because, in turn, these processes affect the structure of the population, the problems of measuring and of ascertaining the nature of these interactions are very complex indeed.[1]

---

[1] For an elaboration of this point see Zelinsky (1966), pp. 15–16.

3 THE MEASUREMENT OF POPULATIONS

Here I shall focus attention first of all on the two basic sets of measurements that the demographer makes.

3.1 The Census

First the demographer draws up a kind of inventory of the population; a list of the characteristics of the individual members of the population, such as age, sex, occupation, race, address, whether native or foreign born, religious affiliation, whether married, single or widowed, place of birth and relationship to the head of the household (e.g. wife, son, daughter, mother, etc.) in which he or she normally lives. Sometimes the demographer seeks more information than this, sometimes less.

In drawing up this inventory, or *census* (the Latin word for count), the demographer is very much aware that the population to which it refers is changing even as he makes a note of it. Individuals are being born, or are dying; losing their jobs or getting new jobs; getting rid of their spouses and, sometimes, getting new ones and so on and so forth. He tries therefore to draw up his inventory, to enumerate his population, over as short an interval as possible – say notionally, at midnight on 25 April 1971 (the date of the most recent United Kingdom census), so as to reduce as much as possible the error of double counting.

3.2 Vital Registration

The second way by which a demographer seeks to measure population is to record the events that cause it to change. The two most important events are births and deaths and these one might term the primary factors of change. Then there are the secondary factors, for example marriages, which obviously affect the number of births, or diseases which affect the number of deaths, or migration (both within and between countries) which affect both.

Many **demographers** are concerned solely with acquiring and manipulating the data provided by the census and by the vital registration system. Increasingly, however, demographers are concerning themselves with what might be called the tertiary factors of population change; tertiary because they act on the population firstly through marriage, disease, or migration, and secondly, at one remove as it were, on births and deaths. The list of these tertiary factors is virtually endless and, in our increasingly complex society, continues to grow at an alarming rate. Here are some, taken at random: the change in the number of jobs; the change in the number of doctors, nurses, hospitals and clinics; the change in the number of women taking the contraceptive pill; the change in the number of houses being built; the change in the number of teachers in schools; the change in wages and taxes; the change in the quantity and type of food available; the change in the amount of coal, oil or electricity produced; the change in the number of cars on the road.

TEST 2

Much of what we shall be examining over the next five weeks is focussed on these secondary and tertiary factors. Before we can understand the impact of these on population change, however, we need to examine the basic or primary ones, which, as I have said, form the core of demographic studies. I shall begin by examining one or two ways in which the demographer examines the structure of populations and then at some ways by which he measures population change.

4 THE STRUCTURE OF POPULATION

4.1 The Sex Ratio

One of the first calculations made by the demographer on receiving the findings of a census is the so-called *sex ratio*. To calculate this, one relates the number of men in the population to the number of women, expressing the answer in terms of 100 or 1,000 women.[1] Thus if a population numbers 950, of which 500 are women and 450 are men, the sex ratio is 450 divided by 500, multiplied by 100, that is to say 90 per 100 women. Sex ratios vary widely between national communities, rural and urban areas, and within different age groups. It is an important measure because not only is it a vital element in any calculations of fertility and mortality trends, but it also has interesting implications for a variety of social and economic matters.

TEST 3

4.2 The Population Pyramid

The age composition of a population is of great interest to the demographer. At most censuses, each individual is asked his precise age, either on his last birthday or on the one subsequent to the census. There is, however, so much misreporting of ages, even in the so-called advanced societies, that the demographer is normally content if he can allocate people to age groups comprising ten, or preferably five years. To show the age composition of a population in a simple and graphic form, the demographer frequently builds a *population pyramid*. The shape of the pyramid not only represents, in a striking fashion, the age composition of the population, but also gives a number of clues as to the processes that have gone into producing the particular age and sex structure of the population.

In building his pyramid, the demographer represents each age group by a horizontal bar. Males occupy the left of this bar, females the right. The actual length of each bar and the point at which it is divided between males and females depends on the number of people in each age group and on their sex. So as to be able to compare, quickly, populations of different sizes, it is usual to represent the number of men or women in each age group according to the proportion they bear to an average 100, 1,000 or 10,000 of the population as a whole. An example is worked out in the Course Notes.

Most populations have a classic pyramid-like structure – like those of Ancient Egypt – that is to say they will be wider at the base than at the top due to the process of attrition, through death, which usually occurs more frequently at the higher than the lower ages.

---

[1] Alternatively one can also express the ratio in terms of men. It is, therefore, very important to check carefully whenever you see a sex ratio.

The pyramid-like structure is, however, not universal and in sizeable populations, those of a whole country or a province for example, one can get a wide variety of shapes, whilst if one looks at smaller populations, such as one finds in an asylum, a college or even a town, one gets a greater variety still.

The pyramid represents the past mortality, fertility and migration experience of the community and can be used to forecast future changes in the population. Here are five pyramids, each representing countries at different stages of demographic development.

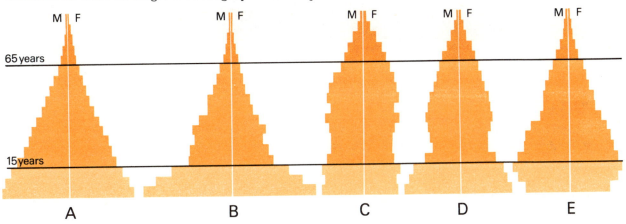

Figure 32.2

Pyramid A represents an underdeveloped country with high mortality and high fertility. Here the burden of dependency is heavy. By that I mean that the number of children is large relative to the number of people in the working age groups who have to support them. One notes, however, that the other dependent age group (the old and retired) is small in such a population, due to high mortality.

Pyramid B represents a population, with high fertility, that has recently experienced a cut in infant and child mortality. Again the burden of dependency is high because of the recent cut in infant and child mortality not being compensated for by an increase in the working population.

Pyramid C which looks rather like an artillery shell represents a population which has experienced low birth and death rates over, say, the past thirty to forty years. In such a community, of those that are born, very few die before they are at least forty years of age; or to put it another way, ninety-five per cent of the population lives to be forty or more years old, which is the situation in most western countries. Here the burden of dependency is low and of the two components of that burden the greater is to be found increasingly at the higher ages.

Pyramid D which again looks rather like an artillery shell this time with a flared mini-skirt represents countries like the United States that had relatively low birth and death rates during the twenty years up to the Second World War but had a sudden upsurge in fertility in the twenty years after it. This latter phenomenon is discussed by Norman Ryder in the *Reader*, pp. 611–16. As few of the newly born have died, such a society has had a growing burden of dependency particularly in the younger age groups.

Finally we have Pyramid E which represents a population that has recently experienced a drastic cut in its fertility, e.g. as Japan has done since the war. This sharp fall in fertility has meant a sharp reduction of the burden of dependency. It is for this reason that most underdeveloped countries are seeking to cut their fertility.

There are, of course, other measures of the structure of the population used by the demographer. But the basic ones are those that we have discussed, for it is the age and sex composition of a population which, taken together, are responsible for the primary processes of change, whilst the total size of the population and the size of its constituent parts is needed by the demographer to measure the rate of change of the population and by other social scientists who endeavour to explain such a change.

TEST 4

5 POPULATION CHANGE

Here the demographer is primarily concerned with the measurement of fertility and mortality over time. The most elementary of these measures are the crude birth and death rates.

5.1 The Crude Birth Rate

The *crude birth rate* is the ratio between the number of births and the population producing those births over a period of time – conventionally fixed at one year. It is called 'crude' because it relates the frequency of births to the entire population and is, therefore, a blunter, less precise measure than one which relates the number of births (or deaths or marriages) to a smaller, more directly relevant portion of the population, such as women of child-bearing age, married and so on. To calculate the crude birth rate one requires three pieces of information. First, one needs the number of births; second, the number of people in the area for which the birth rate is being calculated, and third, when the births occurred, so that one has the time over which the measurement is to be made. Usually we express the crude birth rate as so many births per 1,000 persons per year.

The crude birth rate is then a measure of fertility: the crude death rate, which we calculate in precisely the same way, is a measure of mortality. The difference between the two rates is called the rate of *natural increase*. In most countries the difference between the natural increase of population and the actual increase is small. But, if a country experiences a good deal of immigration or emigration, there can be quite a marked difference. Incidentally, the crude marriage rate is also calculated in this way. That is to say it is the relationship between the size of the population, the number of marriages and the period of exposure which, as we have already said is traditionally taken as one year. These crude rates are the ones that are found most frequently. This is partly because the basic data required for the calculation is relatively easily accessible, and also because the calculation is an easy one.

5.2 The Crude Death Rate

The trouble with crude rates, however, is that they often hide as much about the fertility or mortality or nuptiality – nuptiality is just another way of saying the frequency of marriage – as they reveal. Let me give an example. According to the *United Nations Demographic Yearbook 1969*, the crude death rate for Singapore in 1967 was about six per 1,000: that for Scotland, twelve per 1,000.

Now it is quite obvious that these figures give a misleading impression of the mortality experience of these two countries. The question of accuracy in the statistics obviously plays a part here, since there is little doubt that the Scottish registration system is more reliable

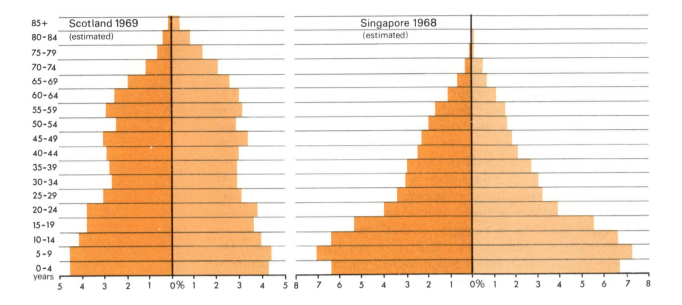

Source: The basic data for Scotland is from 1960 and for Singapore from 1968. It is to be found in the *United Nations Demographic Yearbook 1969*, pp. 174–5 and 182–3.

Figure 32.3 Population pyramids showing the populations of Scotland and Singapore.

than that of Singapore. But the main reason for the difference is not that the Scots, in any particular age group, are more exposed to the chance of death than the inhabitants of Singapore, but that the age composition of the population of the two countries is very different. Scotland has a population pyramid rather like that of type D above, Singapore like type E[1]. And, as noted above, when one calculates the crude death rate, one is unable to take account of differences in the age composition of the population. To get round this difficulty, we try to calculate what are called age specific death rates. We try that is, to get the ages at which people die and relate these to the number of people living at that age. The calculation, once one has got the data, is quite a simple one. Here is an illustration.

Ages (years)	Mid-year Population 1970	Deaths in 1970	Deaths per 1,000 population
20-24	20,000	20	$\frac{20 \times 1,000}{20,000} = 1.0$
25-29	15,000	18	$\frac{18 \times 1,000}{15,000} = 1.2$

And so on for each age group. If we are able to work out age specific death rates for the populations we are interested in, then we can discover the extent to which differences in the crude death rates are the result of differences in the age composition. We can *isolate* one

---

1 Since the fall in fertility is of very recent origin, the structure of the pyramid, excepting the latest cohorts, is like type B.

of the factors affecting mortality. For example, suppose we look again at the mortality experience of Scotland and Singapore. From the crude death rate it would appear that mortality in Scotland is twice that of Singapore, because the rate for the former is twelve per 1,000, for the latter only six. But what would the crude rates look like if both had the same age composition? We can discover this by calculating what is termed the *standardised mortality rate*.

5.3 The Standardised Mortality Rate

To produce one kind of standardised mortality rate we need merely to calculate age specific death rates for each five-year age group of the populations we are interested in. We then decide what our standard population is to be and multiply the age specific death rates that we have calculated by the number of people in each of the corresponding age groups of the standard population. Let us take the Scottish population represented on the population pyramid above as our standard population and work out what the number of deaths would be in Singapore if that country had the same age structure as Scotland. This is done in the following table. The calculation reveals that if Singapore had the same age structure as Scotland and the same age specific death rates as she had in 1968 then her crude death rate would be eighteen per 1,000 – which is some three times as great as she has now, with her present age structure. This shows that the 'population explosion' could become even greater if *age specific* mortality rates in countries like Singapore were reduced to Western levels.

AGE STANDARDIZED DEATH RATE FOR SINGAPORE 1968

Ages	Age specific death rates in Singapore	Standard population (Scotland)	Expected deaths in Singapore
0- 4	9.6	462,400	4,439
5- 9	0.55	471,000	259
10-14	0.52	427,500	222
15-19	0.75	388,800	292
20-24	1.13	395,100	447
25-29	1.26	319,500	403
30-34	1.47	291,300	428
35-39	2.24	295,300	662
40-44	3.89	306,100	1,191
45-49	5.95	335,900	1,999
50-54	10.20	278,700	2,843
55-59	17.95	314,300	5,642
60-64	28.61	289,100	8,271
65-69	46.80	240,100	11,237
70-74	67.40	170,100	11,465
75-79	105.50	112,000	11,816
80-84	281.00	64,300	18.068
Over 85	413.00	32,900	13,588
		Total 5,194,400	Total 93,272

Age standardized death rate for Singapore, 18.0 per 1,000

Source: United Nations Demographic Yearbook 1969 (1970), pp. 174–5, 182–3, 606–7.

5.4 The General Fertility Rate

The search for more refined measures of mortality is paralleled in the case of fertility. The demographer is constantly trying to make his measures more specific by attempting to include in his calculation only those people who are really exposed to the event he is trying to measure. He knows, of course, that births are only produced by people during a certain age period which differs for men and women. It is shorter for women than for men, and since it is women who actually carry the children he may concentrate solely on women above the age of fifteen and below fifty, the child-bearing period. He will miss some women who are exposed to the risks of child-bearing above and below these ages, but they will be few in number.

The first measure the demographer may then calculate is the *general fertility rate*. The word 'general' here, like the word 'crude' is an indication that the demographer is not relating the events (in this case births) to precisely the group of individuals (the actual mothers) who produced them. If the requisite data is available, the calculation is simple. One merely takes the number of births in any particular year and relates this to the number of women in the appropriate age group, which may be fifteen to forty-four years or twenty to forty-nine or fifteen to forty-nine, depending upon the data available and one's particular predilections. Below is an illustration of this calculation.

Women aged 15-44 years on July 1st, 1970	Births in 1970	General fertility rate
800	120	$120 \div 800 \times 1,000 = 150$

5.5 The Child-Woman Ratio

Often, particularly in underdeveloped countries, vital registration data is either unavailable or very unreliable. Since we do not have totals of births we cannot calculate a general fertility ratio. We must depend, therefore, upon the information we can glean from the census, always assuming, of course, that it is available and trustworthy. Using census material we can calculate what is known as the child-woman ratio. Here we take the number of children under, say, five years of age or under one year and relate it to the number of women in the child-bearing age group.

Women aged 15-44 years on July 1st, 1970	Children Under 1 year	Children Under 5 years	Children under 1 year per 1,000 women aged 15-44 years
800	80	320	$80 \div 800 \times 1,000 = 100$
			Children under 5 years per 1,000 women 15-44 years
			$320 \div 800 \times 1,000 = 400$

This particular measure is less satisfactory than the general fertility rate because it reflects not only fertility but also the mortality experience of children in the younger age groups. This can vary very greatly. Young children are particularly vulnerable to a series of infectious diseases. If they are inadequately fed they have little resistance. Thus if one society has greatly reduced the incidence of the major child killing diseases, whilst another society has not been so fortunate, the former might well have a higher child-woman ratio than the latter. This need not necessarily mean that it has higher fertility, just that more of its children survived long enough to be included in the calculation.

5.6 The Total Fertility Rate

Both the general fertility rate and the child-woman ratio are obviously more specific than the crude birth rate, since they do relate births to the persons most likely to be exposed to producing children. However, they still reflect to some extent the age composition of the women within the fertile age group itself. This is an important drawback because we know that women are more likely to have children at certain ages than at others; for example, in some societies they are more likely to have them in their mid-twenties than in their mid-thirties and in almost all societies are more likely to have them at these ages than in, say, their mid-forties. To some extent, of course, the variation will depend upon the age of marriage, since in almost all societies the majority of children are produced by married rather than unmarried women. To overcome these particular snags we try to calculate what is called the *total fertility rate* (TFR). Again, assuming we have the data, the calculation is a simple one. An illustration appears below:

Ages (years)	Births per 1,000 women in each age group	Births per woman in each age group
15-19	15	·0150
20-24	150	·1500
25-29	250	·2500
30-34	180	.1800
35-39	110	·1100
40-44	40	.0400
45-49	25	.0250
	770	·770 x 5 = 3·850

You may wonder why I multiply the figure at the base of the right-hand column by 5. I do so in order to find the total fertility rate for a particular year, since each woman spends five years in the age groups represented in the left-hand column and is, therefore, exposed five times to this particular level of fertility. Ideally, we should calculate the rate for each individual year and then sum each of these rates, as we have done with rates for the five-year age group. But averaging in the first place and then multiplying is usually accepted as being good enough. This measure gives us an indication of the number of children the average woman in the particular population is likely to have, assuming the fertility pattern of each age group[1] remains the same. Furthermore, of course, the measure does remove the distortion produced by variations in the age composition of the women in the fertile age groups.

---

[1] See Ryder's article in the *Reader* on this, especially p. 612.

5.7 Gross and Net Reproduction Rates

Two other measures deserve at least a brief mention. The first of these is the *female gross reproduction rate*. This is a measure designed to indicate the number of female births likely to be produced by a particular population. It is, in other words, the total fertility rate with respect to female births and is usually approximately half the total fertility rate for males and females taken together. One quick way of calculating the gross reproduction rate is to multiply the fertility rate by the proportion of births that are female. For example, if I use the figure produced by the calculation above I would multiply 3.85 × 0.49 (there are almost invariably fewer girls born than boys) which will give us a gross reproduction rate of 1.89.

This is a useful indicator of whether or not a population is able to reproduce itself. If the figure is over 1, then it is possible; if it is under 1, it is impossible. There is, however, a complicating factor,[1] namely, that not all the female children born will survive to the ages at which they will contribute to replacing the population. We must, therefore, estimate the shortfall by examining the mortality experience of the population we are studying. Here is where we draw on the Life Table and by finding out the number of women who can expect to reach, and to pass through the fertile age group, we are able to calculate a more complex measure, known as the *net reproduction rate*. Here is an illustration. We have in column 2 of the table below the births per woman in each group (column 1) as given in our illustration of the total fertility rate on p. 22. By multiplying each of the numbers in this column by 0.49 we arrive at the number of female births (column 3). To calculate the total fertility rate we multiplied each number by 5: that being the maximum number of years each woman could spend in each age group. To get at the net reproduction rate, however, we must multiply the numbers by the *actual* number of years spent in each age group. Obviously this will be smaller the older the age group since the population is progressively reduced by death. Column 4 gives, therefore, the average number of years spent in a particular age group by each of the women who enter it. Multiplying the numbers in column 3 by those in column 4 gives us the expected number of female births per woman. By adding these up we arrive at the female net reproduction rate.

1 Ages	2 Births per woman	3 Female births per woman	4 Average number of years per woman	5 Expected female births per woman
15–19	·0150	·0074	4·2	·0311
20–24	·1500	·0735	4·1	·3014
25–29	·2500	·1225	4·0	·4900
30–34	·1800	·0882	3·8	·3352
35–39	·1100	·0539	3·7	·1994
40–44	·0400	·0196	3·6	·0706
45–49	·0250	·0123	3·5	·0431
	·7700	·3774		1·4708

Net Reproduction Rate   1·4708

[1] Hence the use of the word 'possible' in the previous sentence rather than 'certain'.

TEST 5

5.8 The Application of Demographic Tools

The measures I have discussed are the more elementary ones used by demographers. They each have limitations. Without them, however, one could not begin to discuss population questions. Just how important these, and allied measures are, is well brought out in an article by Norman Ryder, which you will find in the *Reader* (pp. 611–16), under the title 'The Reproductive Renaissance North of the Rio Grande'. In this study Ryder examines the sharp rise in the rate of growth of the United States population which began in the 1940s and continued into the 1950s. This rise was not peculiar to the United States; many western countries had higher growth rates in the decade or so after the Second World War than they had had in the decade that preceded it. The rise in the United States was, however, particularly sharp: so much so that in the 1950s the population there was growing at a faster rate than that of India. The phenomenon which Ryder was examining, and which he labelled 'the reproductive renaissance' was more colloquially called 'the baby boom'. This was because it was widely believed that, at this time, the fall in the size of American families, which had been a continuous one since about 1800, had been reversed. Ryder shows the explanation of the phenomenon was not so simple. That he could do so was because he could draw on the kind of analytical tools we have been examining.

6 THE VERIFICATION OF DEMOGRAPHIC DATA

The previous section has, I hope, shown that in seeking to understand population change, one must know precisely what one is measuring. Ryder's article in the *Reader* confirms that a 'common sense' approach to, for example, an understanding of the 'baby boom' in post-war America is unlikely to get one very near the truth. Only relatively sophisticated statistical techniques can do that. On the other hand, no matter how sophisticated the techniques, unless the demographer can rely on his data, he can do nothing. And in order to verify his data he needs to draw on the insights of other disciplines. What follows are some illustrations of this point, most of which could be elaborated from earlier units of the course.[1]

6.1 The Politics of Demographic Data

It will be apparent from your study of political science in earlier units, that political behaviour is not confined to national institutions such as parliaments and senates. It will be obvious, that in examining the behaviour of any decision-making body, one must examine its unstated as well as its stated aims. This the demographer must do when he receives his data: some of it from national or provincial governments; some of it from agencies of the United Nations; some of it from independent or private organisations, such as the Population Council, or the International Planned Parenthood

---

[1] For a further discussion of the 'pitfalls of official demographic data' see Zelinsky (1966), pp. 17–20.

Federation. One man's view of the credibility of data emanating from one such august body – not necessarily a correct view, of course – is given below.

> There should not be many people now who still believe the extraordinary mis-statement, originally made in 1950, and so widely circulated around the world, that a 'lifetime of malnutrition and actual hunger is the lot of at least two-thirds of mankind'. Why such an obviously erroneous statement should have received such widespread credence is a problem for the social psychologist; a great many people seem to have suspended their normal critical faculties because of the intensity of their belief that the world was over-populated, or needed a world revolution (or both, for some people).
>
> However the World Food and Agriculture Organization (F.A.O.), once sardonically described by *The Economist*[1] as 'a permanent institution devoted to proving that there is not enough food in the world', while recognizing the untenability of the 'two-thirds of mankind' legend, nevertheless sought to harness it in its 'Freedom from Hunger Campaign'. In view of the findings of its Director of Statistics,[2] F.A.O. reduced the proportion of the world's population stated to be in actual hunger to 10–15 per cent, but there were another 35–40 per cent, making a total of half of the world 'malnourished'. F.A.O. apparently succeeded in persuading President Kennedy, Prince Philip, and many lesser dignitaries that half the world was malnourished and most informed opinion believes them. F.A.O. gave no evidence to support their statement, nor even defined 'malnourished' until much later, when they produced their *Third World Survey*. Here they stated (page 9) that people were malnourished unless they lived at the dietary standards of Western Europe, deriving at least 20 per cent of their total calorie intake from animal products, fruits and vegetables, and fats and oils. No evidence at all was given for this standard beyond the statement that 'it is generally agreed'. It was on this proposition, for which no physiological evidence at all was quoted, that half the world was stated to be malnourished. The available medical evidence in fact appears to indicate that most of the inhabitants of Western Europe, far from living at a standard which can be defined as the borderline of malnutrition, are in considerable danger of overnutrition. F.A.O., like many similar organizations, appears to waste enormous sums of money, and devotes much of its energies to political manoeuvres to secure its own perpetuation and aggrandisement. (Clark, 1967, p. 124.)

6.2 The Psychology of Age Reporting

A common characteristic of population censuses, especially those taken among relatively illiterate peoples, is a marked tendency to favour certain figures rather than others in the reporting of ages. In some cases the reasons for this are obvious. For example one would hardly be surprised to find a bunching of the population around the ages at which conscription ends or old age pensions begin. More commonly, however, and more puzzling is the tendency to favour *even* numbers, more particularly those ending in a nought (see over). This phenomenon is usually countered by a variety of statistical techniques, the effect of which is to smooth out the irregularities. Such techniques are not entirely satisfactory, however, since they may hide significant aspects of a population's age distribution. A psychologist could, perhaps, help by casting light on the propensity of individuals to mis-state their ages, either upwards or downwards, and to favour particular ages.

---

1 23 August 1952.

2 Sukhatme, *Journal of the Royal Statistical Society*, Series A, Part IV, 1961.

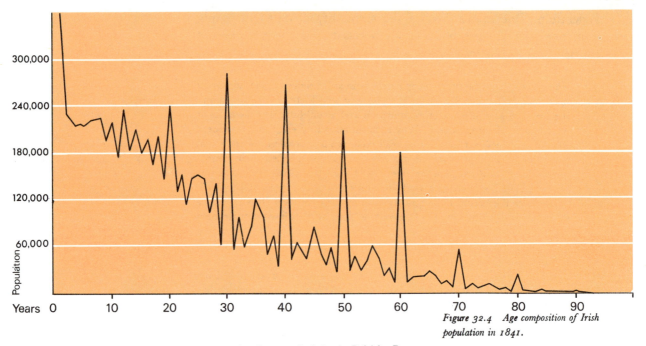

Figure 32.4 *Age composition of Irish population in 1841.*

Source: Reports from Commissioners (1843), *Census of Ireland*, British Parliamentary Papers, XXIV, Plate 5. Dublin, Her Majesty's Stationery Office.

6.3 The Geography of Population Distribution

You will have gathered from Unit 21 that geographers have devised models of urban land use, which enable one to predict, though not, of course, infallibly, the likely distribution of population (itself a reflection of land use) in cities of various kinds. Such a model can be of value to the demographer, especially in dealing with data culled from historical sources or gathered in one of the underdeveloped countries. For in either situation the material is likely to be defective. The question is – how defective? One way of getting an approximate answer is to see the extent to which the actual data fits that which one would expect from the insight provided by the model. The insight is, of course, only approximate, since the model is not an infallible predictor. Nevertheless if there is a gross discrepancy, one must obviously re-examine the data.[1]

6.4 The Economics of Family Formation

This setting-off of actual data against the predictions of a model can also be applied in an economic context. For instance, the economic theory of consumer behaviour that you met with in Unit 10 can obviously be applied to the acquisition of children. They are a type of 'good', possessing both the characteristics of a consumption 'good' as well as those of a capital 'good'. That is to say, children provide the sort of satisfaction one derives from other consumer goods: the pleasure of having offspring is like that from a car, a new dress, a refrigerator, etc. But historically children have also been a form of investment, which paid off in labour (either unpaid in a family concern such as a farm, or a workshop, etc. or paid in some-

---

[1] Zelinsky (1966), pp. 28–33, in his discussion of the physical determinist hypothesis (see Unit 4) gives an interesting example of how in certain limited areas a geographer can 'forecast population size within quite narrow limits, given adequate data on the critical elements in the physical environment and the nature of the links between these elements and population behavior' (p. 29).

one else's business): in a dowry (in the case of boys) or as a form of insurance against old age (often in the case of girls who remained as unmarried and usually unpaid domestic servants in the parental household). In Western industrial societies, children are now almost solely a consumption good – with two cars in the garage what else is there to spend one's money on but a third child! They provide little return (other than the pleasure noted above) and become, with formal education ending later and the age at marriage arriving earlier, a very expensive consumption good. In the underdeveloped world, however, children are still an important investment good, a point that is worth noting and one to which we return on a number of occasions in subsequent units.[1]

It is possible, therefore, to view the 'utility' of children in the way one views that of other commodities and, more speculatively, to predict family size according to the income of the parents. Again the model is by no means infallible, but, given the dubious quality of much demographic data, it is a useful aid to bring to bear upon the reliability of such data. In other words if the data covering, say, the observed distribution of family size bears little or no relation to that postulated by the model, it should be scrutinised with particular care.

6.5 The Sociology of Co-operation

The social scientist who, above all, has a contribution to make to the verification of demographic data is the sociologist or, perhaps more especially in the underdeveloped countries, the social anthropologist. This is so because in underdeveloped countries the taking of a census, or the setting up of a vital registration system is commonly a foreign endeavour – in the literal sense of the term. It is, therefore, of particular value to the demographer to learn from the social anthropologist the kind of bias that is likely to be imported into the census returns or the reporting of births, marriages and deaths. Instances of what has occurred range from the under-enumeration of women or very young children in societies where neither are considered full members of the community; to the misreporting of ages; the boycotting of registrars or census enumerators where these have been selected from despised sub-groups of the population; and the inflation of returns for reasons of prestige or political advantage.[2]

7 CONCLUSION

This unit has focussed on the measurement of population change and on the need for care in ascertaining precisely what is being measured. Such a preoccupation with measurement and conceptual definition is not, of course, peculiar to the world of the demographer. It is shared by all social scientists. If this unit has brought this fact home, its purpose at this point in the course will have been served.

---

[1] See Unit 34, pp. 77–8, Unit 35, p. 108 and Unit 36, p. 158.

[2] For an example of this see Unit 35, p. 129. At the International Population Conference held in London in 1969 a whole section was devoted to the problems of data collection in developing countries. The proceedings of the conference have now been published and though not required for this Foundation Course could well be of interest at a future date. See entry in the bibliography under International Union for the Scientific Study of Population (1971).

ACKNOWLEDGEMENTS

Grateful acknowledgement is made to the following sources for material used in this unit:

Text
Macmillan and Co. for C. CLARK, *Population Growth and Land Use*.

Illustrations
International Bank for Reconstruction and Development for the figure on p. 8; International Planned Parenthood Federation for the figure on p. 7: United Nations for information used in Table 2 in *Demographic Yearbook*, 1969.

BIBLIOGRAPHY

CLARK, COLIN (1967). *Population Growth and Land Use*. London, Macmillan.

INTERNATIONAL UNION FOR THE SCIENTIFIC STUDY OF POPULATION (1971). *International Population Conference*, London 1969. Vols. i–iv. Liege, International Union for the Scientific Study of Population. (The section on data collection in developing countries is in Vol. i, pp. 263–373.)

UNITED NATIONS (1970). *Demographic Yearbook 1969*. New York, United Nations.

Unit 33
Demographic Regions of the Indian Subcontinent

CONTENTS UNIT 33

		PAGE
1	INTRODUCTION	33
2	DEMOGRAPHIC REGIONS IN INDIA	33
	2.1 Unities and Diversities	33
	2.2 The Distribution of Population in the Indian Subcontinent	34
	2.3 Population Density and Population Pressure	37
	2.4 Some Case Studies	38
	2.4.1 Rajasthan	38
	2.4.2 Kerala to Western Mysore	39
	2.4.3 Tamil Nadu to Western Mysore	40
	2.4.4 The Bengal Delta: East Pakistan to West Bengal	41
	2.5 Population and Food Supply	42
	2.6 The Logistic Curve Population Projection	43
3	THE GEOGRAPHY OF MALARIA AND THE POPULATION EXPLOSION	44
	3.1 Introduction	44
	3.2 The Malaria Cycle	44
	3.3 How can the Malaria Cycle be Broken?	46
	3.4 Case Studies of Malaria Eradication	46
	3.4.1 A West Bengal Village	46
	3.4.2 Epidemic Malaria in South Asia	47
	3.4.3 A Case Study from Northern Tanzania	47
	3.4.4 A Successful Eradication Campaign in Kigezi, Uganda	48
	3.4.5 An Unsuccessful Eradication Campaign in Northern Nigeria	48
	3.5 A Global View of Malaria and the Population Explosion	49
	3.6 Conclusion	49
4	THE GEOGRAPHICAL PERSPECTIVE	49
	4.1 Geography and the Population Explosion	49
	4.2 Population Geography and the Geography of *Understanding Society*	50
	4.3 Population Geography and the Discipline of Human Geography	51
	ACKNOWLEDGEMENTS	51
	BIBLIOGRAPHY	52

NOTE:

Students should have Figure 33.6 before them while listening to the relevant radio programme.

The case studies on pp. 42–8 are not included in the radio broadcast.

DEMOGRAPHIC REGIONS OF THE INDIAN SUBCONTINENT

1 INTRODUCTION

In this unit we aim to complement, in a variety of ways, the classic article by Geddes (and its partial up-dating by Learmonth), which is to be found in the *Reader* (pp. 620–42). The first part of the unit offers some additional material covering similar ground to Geddes. The second part deals with the geography of malaria. The writer's study of this topic started in India and we hope you will find it dovetails quite closely into the *Reader* articles. Finally we review this, the last unit from the geographers, in relation to their contribution to the course as a whole. You will find that the set book accompanying this part of the course, Zelinsky (1966), provides a broader perspective, fitting this unit into the study of the world-wide population explosion and into population geography as a whole.

2 DEMOGRAPHIC REGIONS IN INDIA

2.1 Unities and Diversities

In this unit and the associated television programme, we set out first of all to illustrate South Asia as a kind of bubbling cauldron of different – regionally different – responses to population pressure. We then examine this diversity for the law-responsive.[1]

Our television programme starts with this comment from Mrs. Indira Gandhi, Prime Minister of India, on the theme of unity and diversity. It is shot against a background of film, mainly of rural scenes from both humid and semi-arid India.

> India is one country which it is utterly impossible to generalise about. When people come they see any one aspect, and they feel it is the whole India. India is, I suppose all agricultural communities are, basically conservative. It is such a vast country, and there is such diversity of races, of languages, of religions, of customs, not only within the whole of the country, but within each state itself, and with different levels of development. So that in a way it's like very many countries put together, but all the same there is an underlying thread of unity which makes us all very Indian.

Here Mrs. Gandhi was almost echoing her father, Jawaharlal Nehru, who included a section on the variety and unity of India in his book, *The Discovery of India* (1946). This is a semi-autobiographical account of how he came to a new perception of his country and its destiny. The relevance of these comments, from a distinguished father and daughter, to our studies, is that we are here stressing the fact that, for many purposes, generalisations about whole nations may be misleading and we are asking you to consider variations within countries, especially in relation to the population explosion.

---

[1] For the meaning of law-responsive see Unit 4, p. 103.

2.2 The Distribution of Population in the Indian Subcontinent

The rural population density map, reproduced here as Figure 33.1, is a useful complement to the map of demographic regions provided by Geddes in the *Reader* (p. 630). A brief explanatory description of the distribution pattern is given below. It is taken from O. H. K. Spate and A. T. A. Learmonth (1967), *India and Pakistan*, pp. 121–5.

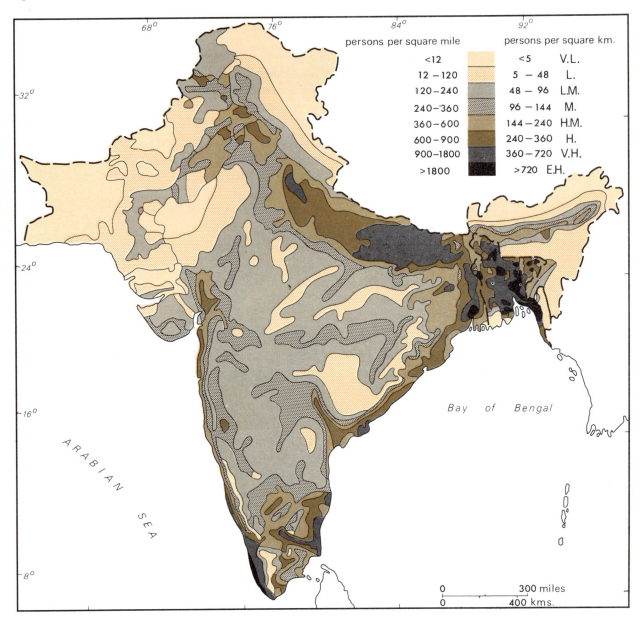

Figure 33.1 From Fig. 4.1, 'Rural Population Density 1961' in O. H. K. Spate and A. T. A. Learmonth, *India and Pakistan*. London, Methuen, 1967. p. 120.

'The density of population is as it were the synthesis of all the geographical phenomena: it expresses eloquently the manner in which man has taken advantage of the land he occupies.' (J. Robert, 'La densité de population des Alpes françaises d'après le dénombrement de 1911', *Rev. de Géographie Alpine* 8 (1920), 124.)

The analysis of a population distribution map which seemed so satisfying in the early 1920s, at least within an area of a relatively homogeneous culture and standards of living, remains a useful exercise for students, though one raising more questions than it solves and inviting further analysis, often impossible for lack of data. The population density map now appears as a beginning rather than an end-product, to be complemented by mapping and analysis of *per capita* income or consumer expenditure, nutritional standards and (in advanced

34

societies) measures of consumer goods and the like to produce estimates of the standard of material living. We shall start with discussion of rural population density and urban population distribution, even if few of the desirable complementary analyses can be more than hinted at for the present. Since Robert wrote, moreover, visual cartographic correlation of the population density map can now be complemented by statistical correlation, even where the base of recording the distribution differs, e.g. as between population and rainfall distributions over areas. Probing attacks using this type of approach for Indian data show that simple statistical analysis breaks down because the relationships involved are too complex and intertwined. Meantime, therefore, we shall use broad generalizations based on visual and subjective analysis.

The excellent map of rural population density in the National Atlas of India (Preliminary Hindi Edition, 1957), on an isopleth basis and in fifteen colours, is based on the 1951 Census and hence is seriously out of date; it is also too complex for easy comprehension. It can, however, provide the starting-point for the compilation of a new and more generalized map of the rural population of the subcontinent, allowing for an over-all intercensal increase of 20 per cent in 1951–61, ignoring as a matter of expediency regional variations: the general pattern is not likely to be significantly altered. For Pakistan the 1961 Census can be directly used; this involves chloropleths based on the smallest administrative units, *tehsils* for West and the smaller *thanas* for East Pakistan. There is therefore an unconformity within the map at the national boundary: in Pakistan the densest shadings are understated, and patches of low populations cutting across administrative boundaries are not well mapped. To avoid irksome repetition of figures in the following discussion, we have given the term 'medium' to densities at around the average for the subcontinent, i.e. about 345 per sq. mile (134 per km^2), and as the key to the map indicates we have given similar descriptive terms to densities ranging from 'extremely high' with over 1,800 per sq. mile (720 per km^2) to 'very low' for densities of under 12 per sq. mile (5 per km^2).

Densities from medium to extremely high, about or above the average density for the subcontinent, cover nearly all the mainly humid coastal lowlands fringing the Peninsular Block; in the Indo-Gangetic Plains they extend westward into semi-arid country and south into the northern edge of the Peninsular Block, while in the northeast of the subcontinent they cover nearly all of East Pakistan and extend into the Assam valley and west into the Damodar valley and parts of the Chota Nagpur plateau. Clearly these areas include much of the most productive land, especially in respect of food crops, and notably much of the rice land of the subcontinent. Within this great stretch of country, variations, reflecting many and diverse factors, include:

1. A belt of high density stretches north from the rice and market gardening lands north of Bombay, through the Baroda area, and after a gap includes a tract of the cotton-growing country tributary to Ahmedabad.

2. High medium densities south of Bombay, in the terrain of low dissected laterite plateaus and drowned valleys, between the Ghats edge and the sea and reaching south beyond Goa.

3. After a narrowing where the forested high plateaus almost meet the sea near Karwar, this belt broadens and includes considerable belts of very high and extremely high densities almost to Kanya Kumari (Cape Comorin); the coastal rice lands of Kerala comprise one of the largest stretches of extremely high rural populations in the subcontinent, declining inland in the low coastal plateaus and the spice garden and plantation country of Kerala and Mysore and then falling very rapidly as the country rises in the almost precipitous Ghats edge, to very low densities.

4. Near Kanya Kumari the narrow coastal lowlands show a sharp change to medium and high medium densities associated with the contrast between perhumid Kerala and semi-arid Tamilnad (and between dispersed-linear settlement pattern in Kerala and nucleated settlements based on tank irrigation); there are patches of high density in the main river plains, rising to very high in the lower Cauvery flood-plain and in the rice lands of the delta and in the peri-urban tract round Madras; it is remarkable that the millet and groundnut unirrigated country includes so much medium to high medium density, but one must allow for the effects not only of tank irrigation of part of the land, but also for narrow belts of well-irrigation along the hillfoot zone flanking the low medium to low density hill tracts of the Pachamalais and Shevaroys, and the southeastern raised rim of the Mysore plateau; the high densities of the

lower Cauvery extend towards the cotton-millet country round Coimbatore and almost link up with those of coastal Kerala.

5. The coastal belt of above-medium densities narrows north of Pulicat lake, then broadens in the Godavari-Krishna delta which is mostly high with very high densities in the Godavari delta; a salient of high densities reaches northwest along the railway line to the coal-mining area of Singareni and Warangal.

6. The inselberg-studded coastal plains of Northern Circars, with rice and sugar-cane alternating with millet and groundnuts, have high densities, almost linking with those of the Orissa (Mahanadi) deltaic rice lands, which in turn links up with the next feature.

7. The great stretch of populations of high to extremely high densities (over 600 per sq. mile or 240 per km^2) in the rice lands of the Bengal delta: West Bengal is generally high, rising to very high and locally to extremely high in a belt following the Hooghly and especially around the Hooghlyside conurbation, and falling to medium in the lateritic Barind tract near the Ganga's turn southeastwards (and extending into East Pakistan); East Pakistan on the other hand is mainly very high, with considerable areas of extremely high densities in the rice and jute tract flanking the lower Padma and Meghna. Islands of lateritic old alluvium, like the Barind or the Madhupur jungle, are mainly of high medium density but might be lower with more sensitive mapping (see introductory paragraph).

8. Most of the Assam valley has high densities, rising to very high in the Nowgong-Tezpur area.

9. The rice lands of the lower Ganga flood-plain tract, including the lower Gandak and Ghaghra, and north to the *terai* on the Nepal border, form a stretch of some 80,000 sq. miles (200,000 km^2) of very high densities, the biggest continuous belt in the subcontinent though the densities are a little lower than those of East Pakistan; densities fall to high medium and locally medium on the cone of the still wandering Kosi.

10. Leaving the main rice lands for the wheat-growing northwest, the upper Ganga and Yamuna plains contain a further very large tract, as much again, of high densities with a tract of very high following the East Yamuna canal tract between Delhi and Meerut; and an aureole of high medium to medium densities surrounds these high densities of the Ganga plains, extending into the northern slopes of the Peninsular block in places, or extending in salients like that of the lower Sŏn valley, and also stretching across the Indo-Gangetic divide.

11. In East Punjab (India) and West Punjab (West Pakistan) and through to the Vale of Peshawar, the long densely settled and intensively cultivated hillfoot tracts of well-irrigation have high densities, but most of the canal tracts high-medium – though more sensitive mapping of West Pakistan data might raise this a little.

12. Nearly all of this continuous stretch of above-medium density covering over half the subcontinent has been in the coastal plains or the Indo-Gangetic plain, and much the greater part has been in rice lands; there remain the more densely peopled parts of the Peninsula, mainly of medium density – the Mysore plateau, rising to high rural densities between Bangalore and Mysore, the long transitional and contact zone east of the forests of the crest zone of the Western Ghats, in Mysore and Maharashtra, rising to high densities in the tobacco growing tract southeast of Kolhapur, much of the tank-irrigation country of Andhra, the upper Godavari valley, the middle Tapti basin and after an interruption a belt stretching east through Nagpur and the Wardha and Wainganga basins to the middle Mahanadi rice-bowl, and the interruption to harsh semi-arid conditions where the Aravallis give a little more rainfall and opportunities for tank building.

The tracts with rural population densities *below* medium (below 240 per sq. mile, 96 per km^2), may be considered more briefly:

1. There are considerable tracts of low and very low densities in the forested hills of the northeast, the forested to glaciated mountains and harsh arid plateaus of the far north, and the great tract of semi-arid to arid conditions from the Thar desert to Baluchistan – this last interrupted by low medium to medium densities of the lower Indus plains (locally probably somewhat higher on more sensitive mapping).

2. Low medium densities stretch from the far north of West Pakistan, and after the higher densities of the Punjab along the wetter eastern part of Rajasthan to inland Gujarat and much of Kathiawad and southern Kutch; thence stretching across about half of the Peninsular Block including much semi-arid country of

variable rainfall and harvests, but also some humid country of rather poor and easily eroded soils in the northeast of the Plateau; within this great swathe of country are several large tracts of very low densities, largely tribal country – parts of the Satpuras, Vindhyas and Bundelkhand, the Kaimur Range, the Maikal Hills and across the higher parts of Chota Nagpur, the Cuddapah ranges of Andhra, the Bastar highlands north of the Godavari delta, linked to the northeast with the 'Eastern Ghats' of Orissa.

TEST 1

2.3 Population Density and Population Pressure

It is a commonplace that population density cannot be equated with population pressure. We do not have all the measurements needed for an adequate assessment of regional variations in population pressure. Nevertheless a pioneer attempt has been made to map population pressure, or, to put it another way, overpopulation and underpopulation in India, by Miss Sen Gupta (Fig. 33.2). Bearing in mind the main points of Geddes's demographic regions, and Learmonth's appraisal of them, the rural population density map (Fig. 33.1) and Miss Sen Gupta's maps (Fig. 33.2), we will now present a number of case studies. These were presented in the television programme and what follows are quotations from the television script.

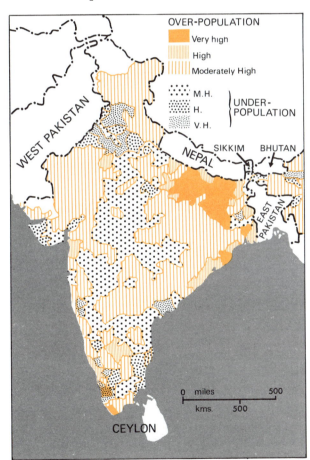 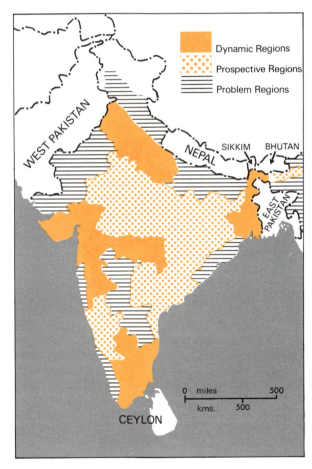

Figures 33.2 (a) and (b) From Fig. 5.7 and Fig. 5.8, 'South Asia' in J. I. Clarke, *Population Geography and the Developing Countries*. Oxford, Pergamon, 1971. pp. 195 and 196.

Here Professor Clarke has drawn on the work of the late Miss Phulrani Sen Gupta, a population geographer of note with the

Census of India. His consideration of her work reads as follows:

> Miss Sen Gupta calculated regional imbalance of population pressure (Fig. 33.2) by use of the formula $I = \frac{P_1 - P}{A}$ where I is the index of population pressure per square kilometre of rural area, P_1 is 'the districtwise derived rural population capable of being supported by the utilized land resources by assuming a constant income per person', P is the actual rural population for each district, and A is the total rural area in square kilometres. Miss Gupta revealed that (a) the areas of very high density (with more than 200 per km) are not always overpopulated, (b) areas with good irrigation facilities and conditions for commercial agriculture are often under-populated, (c) areas of low density (less than fifty per km) are invariably overpopulated, and (d) population pressure is very high in non-irrigated rice-growing areas, especially the middle and east Ganga Plain, the Bhagirathi delta and the Kerala coast. She was also able to divide the country into three types of population-resource regions (dynamic, prospective and problem regions) according to the combined impact of the demographic structure, resource potentiality and levels of socio-economic development upon the supporting capacity of non-agricultural population. Dynamic regions support advanced industrial areas and mainly urban population. Prospective regions have large resource potentials but deficient technology and some socio-economic obstacles to development. Problem regions show little promise, owing to overpopulation, limited resources, lack of transport facilities or other factors. Such a division throws considerable light upon regional disparities, which may well augment in future decades. Certainly, the dynamic regions will be most attractive to internal migrants. One of the tasks of government is to encourage the development of prospective and problem regions.

2.4 Some Case Studies

2.4.1 RAJASTHAN

Here is the wheat country on the edge of the desert. The fields have a system of shallow basins, to trap the sparse and variable rainfall and let it seep into light, sandy soils. The farming is labour-intensive, though it need not always be so. Population density is relatively light, about 150 per square mile – fifty people to the square mile really dependent on farming would be quite dense for good arable country in Britain. Even at 150 per square mile – low by Indian standards – the intensity of application of labour is impressive, at times of harvesting, or weeding, or gleaning grain fallen among the stubble.

In some years the true desert climate sweeps out from the sand dunes of the Thar desert, out across the wheat-growing margins. Here a farming landscape has become for the moment part of the desert. Some people hang on grimly. Others move off with their cattle, hoping to find a place where fitful, patchy rain has made the desert green. This is often a mirage. Even a local proverb says: 'one lean year in three, one famine year in seven'. And the following interview reflects the problem:

INTERVIEWER: How long will it take? How long has he been travelling?
INTERPRETER: He is walking for the last seven days.
INTERVIEWER: How many more days has he got?
INTERPRETER: Eleven more days. Because the cows are all fatigued. So they gradually go out and they starve. They can't work. They are deadly tired.

INTERVIEWER: Could you ask him how many cows he has got left?
INTERPRETER: He says that he has left only two cows, and others have died.
INTERVIEWER: How many cows did he have before?
INTERPRETER: He said about fifty cows he had. He had fifty, now he has only two left. The rest have been taken away by the famine, by the drought. In his life this is the worst drought. He is forty-two years old. [And looks an old man.]

But from the great dam at Bhakra there reaches south the Rajasthan canal to take water from the snows of the Himalaya into the desert. Two hundred of its four hundred miles have been completed. So it is possible for an area like this to move almost overnight from *recurrent crisis*, in Geddes's terms, to *colonisation*.

Canals themselves, however, have their own attendant problems in a hot climate. Overwatering, waterlogging and seepage through the unlined canal bed can give rise to salt-encrusted topsoil over a period of years. Patches like this are extending year by year over North-West India and West Pakistan; remedial measures, such as lining the canals, can be taken, but they are expensive (see Plate 20).

In contrast to the heavy investment involved in large-scale canal irrigation, many villages still water their crops by the more traditional methods of well-irrigation (see Plates 11–13).

Weighted levers and rhythmic movements as men lift water to irrigate crops. Water by the bucketful, flowing along this short, narrow ditch to the fields or gardens. Not much fear of overwatering here. And in the fields hand-digging in labour-intensive cultivation.

On a slightly larger scale is this bigger investment in a large draw-well and ramp to use gravity to help the oxen to pull up a much larger container – in this part of India released by hand – some is taken as drinking water by a woman with her copper pots, perhaps a low-caste water-carrier. But most goes along a rather larger canal to the fields. Much of the country's vegetables and some crops are produced from small-scale types of irrigation. Along the hillfoot zone of the Punjab, well-irrigation tracts provided the immigrants to the original canal colonies of Geddes's article.

In some places diesel or electric engines now lift water and sometimes assist small industries as well. Here agriculture is getting a little more capital-intensive. As in the purely labour-intensive gardens we saw there is an outflow of cash crops to the market.

TEST 2

2.4.2 KERALA TO WESTERN MYSORE

We move from semi-arid Rajasthan to Kerala, on the humid south-west coast of India. High, reliable rainfalls have produced a long period of dependable harvests, which in turn have supported a high natural increase of population. There are traditional industries, for instance – cashew nut processing, tile-making, and the coir industry. Coir is the coarse fibre of the coconut, processed for weaving into mats.

The western half of Mysore state shares many of these features, but inland on the steep edges of the Great Plateau of India, often called the Western Ghats, population is sparser. Here relative stagnation was predominant in Geddes's time, but this has now given way to a transitional type since malaria has come under control.

Here in coastal Kerala, population densities average 1,000 per square mile and even reach 3,000 in some areas. The fishermen go out through the breakers in the evening to spread a great semi-circle of net. Then in the morning it is pulled up the beach by a great concourse of men heaving and shouting in rhythm, while the women and children take the catch from the net. Their houses are among the coconuts, on the sandbar, and the family may till some paddy fields beyond. The temple is tiled with a steep roof against the intensive rains of the long summer monsoon of this part of India. Then relentless south-westerly winds drive much greater waves than these to lash the bay. Behind the fishing villages are the backwaters between the sandbars. There is an ever-increasing road traffic through the land of rural Kerala, but the backwaters remain important highways of commerce; commerce in coconuts and coir, amongst other things. One response to population pressure is to develop small manufactures like the coir industry, again on a labour-intensive basis. The work is mainly manual, but it is very varied. Some of it is hard, even dangerous at times. But other processes call for a skilled eye and a quick hand. And all of this goes into the making of a cheap coconut fibre mat for the kitchen floor.

Inland again, in sheltered well-watered valleys are spice gardens growing pepper, cardomom, betel vine leaves, and the tall, narrow palms of the areca nut, often erroneously called the betel nut because it is usually chewed as a paste with lime, spread on the leaves of the betel vine – and very refreshing it is too.

The hard red-brown areca nuts are one of the most valuable cash crops of India. In the new India of malaria control and the population explosion, one of the most cheering things is to see gardens being opened up again in a valley cut into the steep edge of the Western Ghats, where a few years ago intense endemic malaria caused population decrease, and gardens to be abandoned (Plate 5). Coffee is grown as an important cash crop in South India. Some is grown on peasant plots, but most of it comes from larger-scale plantations, which are increasingly in the hands of Indian capitalists. Tea and rubber are also grown on plantations in the area.

A different response to population pressure on the intermediate plateau has been the growing of cassava, more familiar in its processed state of tapioca. The plateau on which it grows have the tropical soil called laterite, which hardens on exposure like brick.

From the 1920s onwards, cassava has been grown there, thus offering a new food crop in a previously underutilised area.

TEST 3

2.4.3   TAMIL NADU TO WESTERN MYSORE

The State of Tamil Nadu, formerly known as Madras State, has densely peopled ricelands along the eastern coast. Population in this area is over 400 per square mile.

South of Madras the broad skies and the reflections in the paddy fields show the so-called winter monsoon. But as the temperature is over 30° C it is better called the retreating monsoon. Population density is about 700 per square mile. The population trend is of rapid increase following malaria control. This contrasts with

Geddes's *population stagnation* of up to thirty years ago. Rice growing is intensive, using draught cattle and large teams of hire labourers from the large pool of unemployed or underemployed people. This system can be made to yield much more by using improved varieties of seed and artificial fertilisers. This is an area where land reform has not been easy to carry out, and where the increased income from improved agricultural technique has tended to go to the large landholder. This has sometimes contributed to increased social and economic tensions.

Inland, drier areas prevail and these extend into eastern Mysore. Most of this region showed high natural increase in Geddes's survey, as there had been a rapid recovery from the severe famine of 1878, which was just before the period he was considering.

The traditional method of irrigation in this area is from tanks. The tank in India differs from the western concept of a metal container for liquids: there it simply means a small reservoir of water often crudely dammed to provide a controlled outlet to the fields. Different types of tank may also provide drinking water for cattle, a village laundry, or a communal bathing pool.

The next village is in a dry interior valley. Harijans, the formerly outcaste group, often live in separate hamlets on the edge of a South Indian village. During periods of drought, especially when a sequence of dry years succeed each other, migrants from villages and hamlets such as these pour into the State capitals. Bangalore, Madras, and Hyderabad. They usually gravitate to the small shantytown slums squeezed into all-drained hollows between the better houses.

A family's hut was largely destroyed in a storm on the night before I visited them in October 1956. Because there was simply no other alternative permanent accommodation, the parents had to continue occupying their roofless home, whilst their children sheltered with a neighbour.

TEST 4

2.4.4 THE BENGAL DELTA: EAST PAKISTAN TO WEST BENGAL

Bengal, now divided between India and East Pakistan, has high rural densities of between 1,000 and 2,000 per square mile.

The high natural increase of the East in Geddes's time has since been checked by disasters like the 1943 famine and the storm surge from the Bay of Bengal in November 1970. Further north the river floods of the summer monsoon are less devastating, and they do in fact renew soil fertility instead of destroying it with salt. In an attempt to cope with the immense population problem, investment in the delta has been undertaken under the two countries' several economic development plans. East Pakistan has an industrial complex based on the Karnaphuli hydro-electric plant, and modern jute factories like the one at Khulna. West Bengal has great industries like the steel plant at Durgapur on the Damodar river.

But the amount of employment which these developments create has hardly been keeping pace with population pressure in the West Bengal countryside, where the population increase pushes out many people from the poorer groups into the city slums of Calcutta. Rural push rather than urban pull is operating despite the efforts made in economic development plans. The attendant problems of such city migrants is discussed in the television programme associated with Unit 35 by Dr. David Potter, who looks at them from the political scientist's viewpoint.

TEST 5

2.5 Population and Food Supply

If we look at a graph (Fig. 33.3) of food grain production and population trends we can see how, in India at any rate, the two rates of increase have more or less kept pace.[1]

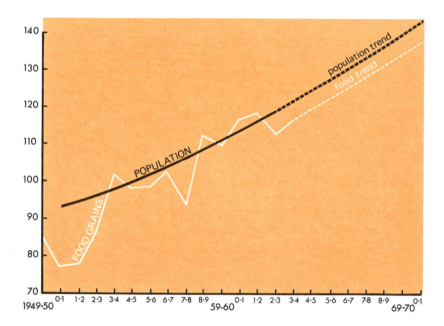

Figure 33.3 India: Trends of Food and Population. Based on figures in S. E. Johnson, *India's Food Situation and a Look Ahead* (Report to Ministry of Food and Agriculture, 1963). From O. H. K. Spate and A. T. A. Learmonth (1967), *India and Pakistan*. London, Methuen. p. 281.

This graph shows how food production has sagged below the rate of increase of population in years of bad harvests, with occasional peaks above the less volatile population graph, in years of good crops. Since the years plotted from the fairly precise estimates, harvests were poor to disastrous in the mid-60s but good in the late 60s and 1970. The base year (index no. 100) is 1955.

Between 1951 and 1961 the rate of population increase rose from 1.1 per cent to 2.2 per cent. This rise largely wiped out the benefits hoped for under the first two Five Year Plans. In the mid-60s a run of bad harvests, along with international tensions, caused a diversion of development funds from industrial development into the agricultural sector.[2]

So India's plans to improve the country's standard of living have been interrupted and checked by increasing population pressure. But if new and improved techniques of family planning begin to curb the birth rate drastically as it is hoped they might, the present population explosion may well be levelling off by the year 2000, so that a logistic curve of the period may approximate to Figure 33.4.[3]

1 See also Unit 35, pp. 114–16.

2 See below, Unit 34, pp. 90–9.

3 See Unit 36 for a discussion of the likelihood of this happening, especially pp. 166–8.

2.6 The Logistic Curve Population Projection

If a population is rapidly increasing after a relatively static period (whether of Geddes's 'stagnation' or 'recurrent crisis' type), one possible population projection would be to fit a curve, mathematically, with the closest possible fit to all the points at which the population has been measured, and to assume that after a period the rate of increase will become less, until population stability is attained at some higher figure. If the figures show that a decline in *rates* of increase has begun, the flattening out at the top of the curve may have fair forecasting validity. But if there is no such slackening in the rates increase, then the period before it may begin is a matter of guesswork. Figures 33.4 and 33.5 are two presentations using the logistic curve idea. We have included expanded captions which may help you if these ideas are unfamiliar to you.

The logistic or logarithmic curve applied to population increase is one in which after attaining a peak rate of increase the rate tends continually to fall off. This application to human population growth was first proposed by a Belgian, Verhulst, in 1858. As in many of the models of population growth analogies have been applied from animal populations, but in these there is conflicting evidence – some supporting this model, some suggesting that conditions of overcrowding and poor nutrition, fertility is increased, at least up to a certain point. In human populations the problems are complex, but there is some evidence that population growth tends to fall off as standards of living improve beyond a point, depending on various cultural variables. Annotations on Davis's graph suggest links with Geddes's viewpoint, and Figure 33.5 gives another view of demographic change.

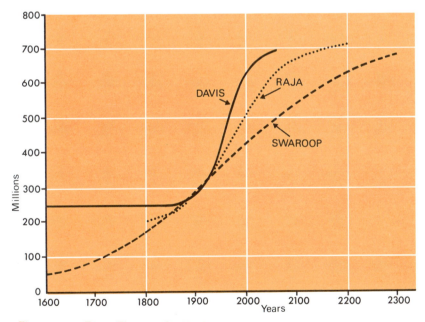

Figure 33.4 From Fig. 55, G. K. Davis, *The Population of India and Pakistan*. Princeton, N.J., 1951. appendix.

Figure 33.5 overleaf From Fig. 18.1, R. Chung, 'Space-time diffusion of the transition model: the twentieth-century patterns', in G. J. Demko, H. M. Rose and G. A. Schnell, *Population Geography: A Reader*. New York, McGraw-Hill, 1970, p. 222.

Figure 33.6 Malaria, Interlocking Cycles.

This diagram complements the logistic graph of Figure 33.4. It is sometimes referred to as the 'population cycle'.

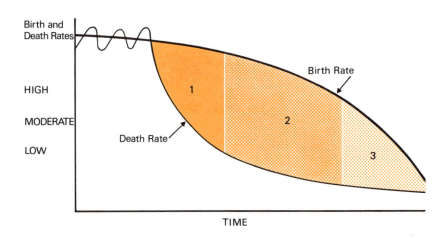

COMPONENTS OF THE DEMOGRAPHIC TRANSITION

Stage 1. High birth rate   (Crude birth rate over 30)
         High death rate   (Crude death rate over 15)

Stage 2. High birth rate   (Crude birth rate over 30)
         Rapidly declining death rate (Crude death rate under 15)

Stage 3. Low birth rate   (Crude birth rate under 30)
         Low death rate   (Crude death rate under 15)

3 THE GEOGRAPHY OF MALARIA AND THE POPULATION EXPLOSION

3.1 Introduction

You may well wonder why we should have included a discussion of the geography of malaria in a course on *Understanding Society*. We think it is relevant to this last block of five units on the population explosion because the control or eradication of malaria over large parts of the tropical and sub-tropical world is often thought to be a very important factor in the population explosion. It is, however, by no means the only one, and everywhere coincides with other important social and economic developments.[1] We begin with a discussion of the malaria cycle.[2]

3.2 The Malaria Cycle

The malaria cycle as a whole consists of three interlocking cycles.

CYCLE 1

The malaria parasite *Plasmodium*, in the Protozoa. The genus include species parasitic on birds, apes, monkeys, etc. The four human malaria parasites are *P. vivax*, *P. falciparum*, *P. malariae* and *P. ovale*. Both man and mosquito are essential to the parasite, for particular stages of its life cycle must take place in the mosquito, others in man, and it can have no independent existence at least outside the laboratory. (Strictly, man and *Anopheles* are alternate hosts, but the latter is commonly referred to as the vector.)

1 On this see Unit 35, p. 119.
2 See Unit 4, p. 99. On the systems approach.

CYCLE 2

The vector mosquito *Anopheles*, a genus of many species with different preferences in breeding and resting places and feeding habits. For instance some rest in houses, some in trees, etc. For the malaria cycle to continue an adult female mosquito has to suck infected blood. She must then live for about two weeks during which the parasite goes through various stages of development in her body. She must then suck blood from a susceptible person, discharging minute early-stage parasites (sporozöites) into his blood from its salivary glands. Mathematically or statistically-minded students may think that there is ground here for some probability calculation; this has indeed been worked on from Sir Ronald Ross (1910) to George Macdonald (1957).

CYCLE 3

Man. For the cycle to continue (a) susceptible man and (b) infected man must be in fairly close contact, and in specific contact through the vector mosquito. We shall return to consider man in more detail.

TEST 6

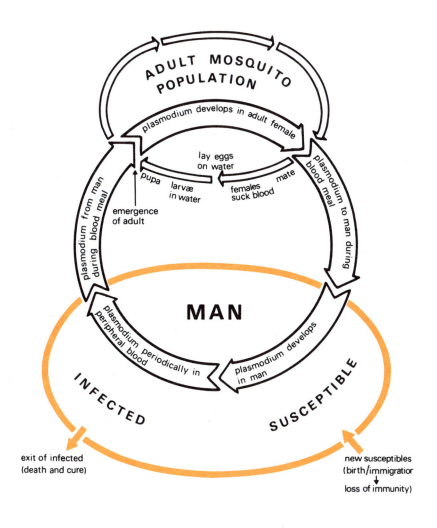

Figure 33.6 Malaria, Interlocking Cycles.

3.3 How can the Malaria Cycle be Broken?

(a) By destroying the larvae hatching from eggs laid on a water surface and swimming up and down in the water in search of food and oxygen.

(b) By attacking the adult form, especially the female resting after a blood meal, often with an insecticide.

(c) A future possibility is by releasing large numbers of males, sterilised by subjecting them to particular radiations, so that they swamp the natural, fertile males in the search for virgin females, so almost preventing breeding.

(d) Protect susceptible man by prophylactic drugs, like war-time mepacrine or modern chloroquine; *mass* chemoprophylaxis can now be attained.

(e) Treat infected man by drugs, from quinine taken from cinchona bark to modern chemical compounds; *mass* chemotherapy can now be done. Mark these attack points on your copy of Figure 33.6

3.4 Case Studies of Malaria Eradication

3.4.1 A WEST BENGAL VILLAGE

Here Malaria used to be hyperendemic. That is to say it was constantly present, as against being epidemic, or only intermittently present. The local vector, *Anopheles philippinensis*, prefers to breed in clean but still water. The 'dying delta' is very rich in ponds, often inadvertently caused by man, e.g. in road and rail embankments and in 'borrow pits' (caused by brickmaking) as well as in mud walls and on house platforms. So mosquitoes are numerous and man-mosquito contact intimate in this crowded land. What were the demographic effects of hyperendemic malaria? Live births were somewhat lowered by increased abortions (other diseases contributing). Babies might have some congenital immunity, fading after a few months, and giving way to heavy malarial infections with severe illness and many deaths among older babies, toddlers and young children. Survivors to adult life had some immunity, but the prevalent parasite, *Plasmodium vivax*, is always associated with severe indisposition even in these circumstances. (This might argue that it is relatively recently evolved as a human disease, perhaps having evolved from a zöonosis, an animal disease like monkey malaria into which man somehow blunders. Natural as distinct from laboratory transmission of simian malaria to man has been recorded twice within the last few years: the first observations known to science.)

Today malaria control has been established, followed quickly by malaria eradication. The mosquito was house-haunting, so that the people only had to give spray teams access to houses and cattle sheds, rather than adopt a regular regime of chemotherapy.

Population stagnation, to use Geddes's term, has been succeeded by increases of over one per cent per annum – less than in many parts of India but increasing the already severe population pressure. The increase would have been more but for the fact that cholera and smallpox, though reduced, have not been mastered, nor the millenial scourge of dysentery and the newer ones of tuberculosis and venereal disease. The latter is particularly associated with the return home of young men, from a spell of wage-earning in Calcutta. And malnutrition, already present, has probably increased, especially in the economically vulnerable landless groups.

TEST 7

3.4.2 EPIDEMIC MALARIA IN SOUTH ASIA

Elsewhere in India, wet forest tracts have hyperendemic malaria with similar demographic effects in a sparser population, but the vector mosquitoes breed in clear, fast-flowing jungle streams, though the adults are house-haunting. A breeding place of such a vector, *Anopheles fluviatilis*, is seen in Plate 1.

In all middle India, again, the chief vector is a still-water breeder, *Anopheles culicifacies*, able to adapt to an enormous range of water bodies very quickly after the onset of rains, and to increase enormously in numbers in a year of heavy monsoon rainfall. It can probably expand its territory also by sizeable migrations with the assistance of the winds, in wet years. It is house-haunting and the great epidemic malaria vector. In epidemic malaria the incidence and demographic effects are quite different from endemic malaria. There is much severe illness and many deaths in all age groups of the population. Casualties among men and women at the peak of their economic and family functions cause economic and demographic dislocation and many vulnerable orphans are left. There are peaks of mortality however – among the very young who have been born since the last epidemic and so have no immunity, and among the very old – just as in an influenza epidemic in Britain.

TEST 8

3.4.3 A CASE STUDY FROM NORTHERN TANZANIA

This study is to illustrate some of the problems that have made Africa, especially tropical Africa, much more difficult for malaria eradication programmes than most other parts of the tropics.

Our tribal village is in hyperendemic malaria country which is also rainforest country. The late infant, toddler and child mortality are as described from India, but the malaria parasite here is mainly *Plasmodium falciparum*, which may cause less severe illness among survivors to adult life than the *P. vivax* of West Bengal. (This might argue that *P. falciparum* was earlier evolved as a human disease than *P. vivax*.) The two great and complementary vectors of tropical Africa, *Anopheles gambiae* and *A. funestus*, have for centuries been very efficient vectors of malaria. *A. funestus* has been above all the breeder in permanent water-bodies, *A. gambiae* the vector with extraordinary powers of adaptation, seasonally and from year to year, to all sorts of water-bodies, including temporary pools that last only long enough for the mosquito eggs to hatch and the larvae to pupate. In this they somewhat resemble *A. culicifacies* in India, but unlike that vector, or *A. funestus*, *A. gambiae* suffered only a temporary setback on being attacked by the spraying of houses with insecticides like DDT. House-haunting strains within the species were wiped out, but the species also included strains breeding and living as adults in a very wide variety of forest environments. These are inaccessible to any conceivable form of larvae or adult control, except possibly the technique of releasing great numbers of sterilised males but the perfecting of this technique belongs to the future. Meantime versatility in the choice of breeding place may mean the actual replacement of *A. funestus* by *A. gambiae*. On the other hand, the great range of forest resting places may mean that after sucking infected blood, and developing human malaria parasites in their body, many mosquitoes may next suck blood from a monkey or other forest mammal, and not from a man. But their numbers are so vast that they seem to be very efficient vectors. They seem to like human blood, and as over much of tropical Africa cattle cannot be kept, because of tsetse fly which carry animal disease as well as human sleeping sickness, the people are denied a common 'screen' and an alternative source of mosquito prey.

TEST 9

3.4.4 A SUCCESSFUL ERADICATION CAMPAIGN IN KIGEZI, UGANDA

In the radio broadcast, a BBC recording of Dr. Julian de Zulueta is used to set out some features of this campaign, which successfully overcame the difficulties, using a combination of house spraying with preventive and curative drugs. Without withholding all due credit for this success, we asked Dr. R. M. Prothero for some critical assessment. He pointed out that the people had recently been resettled in the area, their number and locations were known more precisely than is often true in Africa, and there a widely accepted tribal authority was still vested in the chiefs, who supported the campaign.

TEST 10

3.4.5 A TROUBLED ERADICATION CAMPAIGN IN NORTHERN NIGERIA

A campaign against malaria in Northern Nigeria some years ago under Professor L. J. Bruce-Chwatt met with unexpected difficulties. He found that seasonal migration was causing some people to miss the campaign, and that returning migrants might bring back fresh infections, ready to flare up if the vector returned. He consulted Dr. R.M. Prothero, a geographer who had worked on migration in the area, and who later worked for WHO on this problem on a wider canvas (see Prothero 1965). We asked Dr. Prothero (in the radio programme) to pin-point the use of geography in this unusual context.

Prothero was clear that the geographer could start by a quite simple mapping of movements, but precise and comprehensive in areal and seasonal coverage. Even this simple step is often neglected in malaria projects. Further analysis on the types and causes of migration clearly has its part to play in understanding what kind of arrangements can be made to deal with the problem in relation to malaria eradication. He mentioned even the uses of remote sensing from artificial satellites as a means of keeping track of pastoral nomads, e.g. in the Horn of Africa region. More generally, Prothero believes that of the three factors in the malaria cycle man is the one most neglected by the medical men and entomologists who normally dominate eradication teams.

TEST 11

3.5 A Global View of Malaria and the Population Explosion

Three underdeveloped countries, Ceylon, British Guiana (now Guyana) and Mauritius, were very early in malaria control. Almost simultaneously, their rate of growth went up suddenly to about three per cent per annum. This means a very high growth rate by world standards, especially if standards of living are to be improved. India had a rather lower rate, about 2.2 per cent per annum but her very large numbers mean that she is having to cope with an annual increase of thirteen million people at a time when she is also trying to improve standards of living through her Five Year Plans. Population increase, in fact, largely wiped out the benefits hoped for under the Second and Third Five Year Plans. But is malaria control the only factor of change?

We asked Dr. Bruce-Chwatt (again in the radio programme) if malariologists could be, as it were, blamed for the population explosion. He gave some figures. About fifteen years ago some 1,250 million people lived in malarious areas, about 250 million cases of malaria occurred annually, and about 2.5 million died. Now there are about 100 million cases a year, with under a million deaths. So very roughly about fifteen million haven't died from malaria in the last decade as a result of malaria control, a large figure but not in proportion to the 500 million people by which the world population has increased in that time.

TEST 12

3.6 Conclusion

Malaria control is associated with a sharp movement in the rate of population increase in many areas, but the causes appear to be multiple. So as far as malaria is a brake on population increase, the student is asked to differentiate between the differing demographic, social and economic effects of endemic as compared with epidemic conditions. And in considering the differing success of malaria control campaigns, e.g. as between South Asia and Africa, to consider all three factors in the malaria cycle: the malaria, anopheles mosquito and the differing habits of its many species; the malaria parasite, *Plasmodium* and its many species alternately parasitic on man and on a mammalian host; and lastly man, infected man and susceptible man – our proper and a neglected study!

4 THE GEOGRAPHICAL PERSPECTIVE

In this final section we shall endeavour to relate the unit, first to the other units in this part of the course; second, to the other geography units in the course as a whole and finally, on a much broader canvas, to the discipline of human geography.

4.1 Geography and the Population Explosion

This unit has sought to underline, this time in a spatial setting, one of the main points of Unit 32: namely, the need to refine as much as possible one's analyses of social phenomena. In Unit 32 this was illustrated by considering the demographer's efforts to measure fertility and mortality. Here we have sought to delineate regional variations in population growth, as well as the varying patterns of disease and measures against it, in the case of one disease – malaria.

Integration with Unit 34 is somewhat less close, largely because to develop more fully the closely related theme of economic development in the countries of South Asia would have carried the unit beyond the scope of a week's work. That the links are there, awaiting further study, should, however, be apparent.[1]

This unit, like Unit 35, has tried to expose the fallacies implicit in some of the generalisations made about population change, though in the process it may well have added a few to the corpus of loose statements. Again like Unit 35 the population geographer stresses the complexity, the interrelatedness of population phenomena and the wide range of choices open to man.

Finally the Geddes article in the *Reader*, one of the main foci of this week's work, contains an explicit, if some think naïve, excursion into interdisciplinary studies – especially in the direction of social psychology. The scientific study of innovation, the especial concern of Unit 36, reciprocates this interest, since its setting is the bubbling cauldron of different responses to population pressure that is India today and which we have tried to illustrate here.

4.2 Population Geography and the Geography of *Understanding Society*

To some extent this week's work is designed to be a partial synthesis of the geographical content of the course as a whole. Here then are some pointers to the links with earlier units. In Unit 4, the networks and systems approach, much developed in Units 19–22, is useful whenever population movements are considered dynamically over time. The discussion of physical determinism is also of relevance. Geddes regarded it as a duty to study the relationship between the physical environment and the total social environment. You will find, therefore, that he was exploring a physical determinist hypothesis. He was by no means preaching the physical determinist doctrine of the control of man by the physical environment, nor selecting his evidence in a biased way to prove a physical determinist hypothesis. The techniques he used were partly of his time and partly a little ahead of it. The Geddes paper can be seen, in fact, as an early use of a theoretical model, when he sets a theoretical population curve against the actual population as shown in the census, in order to show the variability in the process of population change. He also used quantitative methods in a way that was at the time new and exciting to geographers.

Links with Units 19–22, apart from the model approach, are not strong chiefly because they deal mainly with developed countries, and the examples from underdeveloped countries are of a different scale from those in the present unit. All the same it is by no means difficult to see cross-links, explicit or implicit, between the population geography and social, economic and political geography: for example, the effects of the change in the rate of population increase on India's Five Year Plans, to some extent regionally differing in impact. There are also some links with Unit 23 – for instance the post-Partition migrations referred to there explain some features of the population geography.

[1] Compare for instance pp. 42–3.

4.3 **Population Geography and the Discipline of Human Geography**

In Unit 4 we suggested that population geography is logically part of social geography, but there are reasons for regarding it as one of the main channels of synthesis within the discipline.[1] For it has some links with social, economic and political geography and indeed with historical geography. Over the past forty years or more population geography has also been used as a means of synthesis in regional studies. It certainly does involve these various geographies and even beyond them it joins up with such disciplines as sociology, economics and political science as well as with demography. It is perhaps appropriate, therefore, that we end on this note – always remembering, of course, that the placing of a branch of knowledge within a discipline or between disciplines is more usually a matter of academic convenience than of academic substance!

1 See the comment of Zelinsky (1966) (cited in a set book, p. 3) 'That population geography should be a major autonomous branch of the larger field of geography'. Also the quotation from Robert on p. 34.

TEST 13

ACKNOWLEDGEMENTS

Grateful acknowledgement is made to the following sources for material used in this unit:

Text

Methuen & Co. Ltd. for O. H. K. SPATE and A. T. A. LEARMONTH, *India and Pakistan*.

Illustrations

MRS. J. GEDDES for Plates 7–9; A. T. A. LEARMONTH for Plates 1–6 and 10–12; McGraw-Hill Book Company for Fig. 33.5 in G. J. DEMKO, H. M. ROSE and G. A. SCHNELL, *Population Geography*; Methuen & Co. Ltd. for Figs. 33.1 and 33.3 in O. H. K. SPATE and A. T. A. LEARMONTH, *India and Pakistan*; Pergamon Press Ltd. for Fig. 33.2 (a) and (b) in J. I. CLARKE, *Population Geography and the Developing Countries*; Princeton University Press for Fig. 33.4 in G. K. DAVIS, *The Population of India and Pakistan*.

BIBLIOGRAPHY

Note: This list consists of references and acknowledgements NOT prescribed as part of the reading for this unit, except for the works marked *.

CHUNG, R. (1970). 'Space-Time Diffusion of the Transition Model: the Twentieth Century Patterns,' pp. 220–39, in G. J. Demko, H. M. Rose and G. A. Schnell, *Population Geography: A Reader*. New York, McGraw-Hill.

CLARKE, J. I. (1965). *Population Geography*. Oxford, Pergamon.

CLARKE, J. I. (1971). *Population Geography and the Developing Countries*. Oxford, Pergamon.

*GEDDES, A. (1947–48). 'The Social and Psychological Significance of Variability in Population Change with examples from India, 1871–1941,' *Human Relations*, 1, pp. 188–205. Also reproduced in our Reader *Understanding Society*, Macmillan, 1970, pp. 620–36.

*LEARMONTH, A. T. A. (1966). 'Selected Aspects of India's Population Geography', *Australian J. Pol. & Hist.*, 12, pp. 146–54, amended as 'India's Population Geography during an era of change', in our Reader *Understanding Society*, Macmillan, 1970, pp. 636–42.

MACDONALD, G. (1957). *The Epidemiology and Control of Malaria*. London, Oxford University Press.

PROTHERO, R. M. (1965). *Migrants and Malaria*. London, Longmans.

ROSS, R. (1910). *The Prevention of Malaria*. London, John Murray.

SPATE, O. H. K. and LEARMONTH, A. T. A. (1967). *India and Pakistan*. London, Methuen.

TREWARTHA, G. T. (1969). *A Geography of Population: World Patterns*. New York, Wiley.

WILSON, M. G. A (1968). *Population Geography*. Melbourne, Nelson.

*ZELINSKY, W. (1961). *A Prologue to Population Geography*. Englewood Cliffs, N.J., Prentice-Hall.

POSTSCRIPT

THE CENSUS OF INDIA 1971 – PROVISIONAL TOTALS

Since the first bulletin from the Census of India has come to hand just as this unit is going to press, we are including some of the first tables. The most crucial, from the viewpoint of the population explosion, is Table 2. Taking the figures for States only, the lowest third have grown in the decade 1961–71 by 19.7 per cent to 23.9 per cent, the middle third by 25.0 per cent to 27.6 per cent and the top third by 28.0 per cent to 39.6 per cent. So on this evidence, the regionally patchy picture of Geddes's time has further receded, the population explosion is even more universal. On the other hand

TABLE 1

TOTAL POPULATIONS AND POPULATION DENSITIES OF THE STATES, UNION TERRITORIES AND OTHER AREAS OF INDIA, 1971

Ranking in 1971	States, Union Territories and Other Areas in order of Population size	Population 1971	Population per square kilometre
	INDIA	**546,955,945**	**182**
1.	Uttar Pradesh	88,299,453	300
2.	Bihar	56,387,296	324
3.	Maharashtra	50,295,081	163
4.	West Bengal	44,440,095	507
5.	Andhra Pradesh	43,394,951	157
6.	Madhya Pradesh	41,449,729	93
7.	Tamil Nadu	41,103,125	316
8.	Mysore	29,224,046	152
9.	Gujarat	26,660,929	136
10.	Rajasthan	25,724,142	75
11.	Orissa	21,934,827	141
12.	Kerala	21,280,397	548
13.	Assam	14,857,314	149
14.	Punjab	13,472,972	268
15.	Haryana	9,971,165	225
16.	Jammu & Kashmir	4,615,176	—
17.	Delhi	4,044,338	2,723
18.	Himachal Pradesh	3,424,332	62
19.	Tripura	1,556,822	149
20.	Manipur	1,069,555	48
21.	Meghalaya	983,336	33
22.	Goa, Daman and Diu	857,180	225
23.	Nagaland	515,561	31
24.	Pondicherry	471,347	982
25.	North-East Frontier Agency	444,744	—
26.	Chandigarh	256,979	2,723
27.	Andaman & Nicobar Islands	115,090	14
28.	Dadra & Nagar Haveli	74,165	151
29.	Laccadive, Minicoy & Amindivi Islands	31,798	994

more detailed mapping may bring out more residuals of the differentiated picture of the past. Mapping the Statewise data for what they are worth, rates are relatively low in South-Eastern India and in most of the Ganga plains, medium in most of the western and north-eastern Peninsula and into West Bengal despite the long history of immigration, including refugees, from East Pakistan, so that the indigenous trend there is probably one of relatively low increase. The high rates are in industrial Gujarat and Madhya Pradesh perhaps representing freedom there from the current crises of Geddes's work, and in a group of mountainous States in the North which have rather small populations. Here, Himachal Pradesh is the exception, with relatively low rates.

Rates of urban growth have increased in this decade as compared

TABLE 2

THE GROWTH OF POPULATION IN THE STATES, UNION TERRITORIES AND OTHER AREAS OF INDIA, 1951-61 AND 1961-71

India/State/Union Territory and Other Area	% growth rate of population	
	1951—1961	1961—1971
INDIA	+21·64	+24·57
STATES		
1. Andhra Pradesh	+15·65	+20·60
2. Assam	+35·06	+33·51
3. Bihar	+19·77	+21·38
4. Gujarat	+26·88	+29·21
5. Haryana	+33·79	+31·36
6. Himachal Pradesh	+17·87	+21·76
7. Jammu & Kashmir	+9·44	+29·60
8. Kerala	+24·76	+25·89
9. Madhya Pradesh	+24·17	+28·04
10. Maharashtra	+23·60	+27·16
11. Mysore	+21·57	+23·90
12. Nagaland	+14·07	+39·64
13. Orissa	+19·82	+24·99
14. Punjab	+21·56	+21·00
15. Rajasthan	+26·20	+27·63
16. Tamil Nadu	+11·85	+22·01
17. Uttar Pradesh	+16·66	+19·73
18. West Bengal	+32·80	+27·24
UNION TERRITORIES AND OTHER AREAS		
1. Andaman and Nicobar Islands	+105·19	+81·11
2. Chandigarh	+394·13	+114·36
3. Dadra and Nagar Haveli	+39·56	+27·95
4. Delhi	+52·44	+52·12
5. Goa, Daman and Diu	+5·14	+36·78
6. Laccadive, Minicoy and Amindivi Islands	+14·61	+31·90
7. Manipur	+35·04	+37·12
8. Meghalaya	+25·97	+32·02
9. North-East Frontier Agency	—	+32·14
10. Pondicherry	+16·34	+27·71
11. Tripura	+78·71	+36·32

with 1951-61 (Table 4) judging by the evidence of the major cities and conurbations. Here increases of between 31 per cent and 54 per cent, all above the national average rate of increase, have occurred. Urban pull certainly exists for particular groups and in particular employment markets, e.g. for certain types of industrial employees, but it would be over-optimistic to regard most of the movement as due to an increased demand for labour in urban areas. More must still be due to rural push, as population pressure increases in the countryside.

The total population has increased from 439 millions in 1961 to 547 millions in 1971, an increase of 108 millions or 24.6 per cent, over the decade. That this has been accomplished, despite a run of bad harvests, without major and uncontrolled famine, is a remarkable tribute to both governmental and international concern. That general standards of living may have improved even marginally, despite the interruptions to the Five Year Plans is remarkable. It

TABLE 3

PERCENTAGE OF THE POPULATION WHO ARE LITERATE IN THE STATES, UNION TERRITORIES AND OTHER AREAS OF INDIA, 1961 AND 1971

Ranking in 1971	State/Union Territory/Other Area	Literacy rate in 1971	Literacy rate in 1961
	INDIA	**29·35**	**24·03**
1	Chandigarh	61·24	51·06
2	Kerala	60·16	46·85
3	Delhi	56·65	52·75
4	Goa, Daman & Diu	44·53	30·75
5	Andaman & Nicobar Islands	43·48	33·63
6	Laccadive, Minicoy & Amindivi Islands	43·44	23·27
7	Pondicherry	43·36	37·43
8	Tamil Nadu	39·39	31·41
9	Maharashtra	39·06	29·82
10	Gujarat	35·70	30·45
11	Punjab	33·39	26·74
12	West Bengal	33·05	29·28
13	Manipur	32·80	30·42
14	Mysore	31·47	25·40
15	Himachal Pradesh	31·32	21·26
16	Tripura	30·87	20·24
17	Assam	28·74	29·19
18	Meghalaya	28·41	18·47
19	Nagaland	27·33	17·91
20	Haryana	26·69	19·93
21	Orissa	26·12	21·66
22	Andhra Pradesh	24·56	21·19
23	Madhya Pradesh	22·03	17·13
24	Uttar Pradesh	21·64	17·65
25	Bihar	19·97	18·40
26	Rajasthan	18·79	15·21
27	Jammu & Kashmir	18·30	11·03
28	Dadra & Nagar Haveli	14·86	9·48
29	North-East Frontier Agency	9·34	7·13

would appear that family-planning campaigns have had only local effects so far, and that only in particular groups is there a marked extension of the felt need for smaller families. More than ever co-ordinated effort, rather than family planning campaigns alone, are required in order to improve the standards of living at a faster rate, so that the conditions for a slower rate of population increase are attainable, say by the turn of the century.

TABLE 4

CITIES OF INDIA WITH POPULATIONS OF ONE MILLION AND OVER, 1971

Name of City/State	1971 Provisional Population	
	Persons	Percentage increase 1961-71
1. Calcutta Urban Agglomeration (*West Bengal*)	7,040,345	c. 50
2. Greater Bombay (*Maharashtra*)	5,931,989	43·1
3. Delhi Urban Agglomeration	3,629,842	53·9
(*a*) Delhi Municipal Corporation (U)	3,279,955	
(*b*) New Delhi Municipal Committee	292,857	
(*c*) Delhi Cantonment	57,030	
4. Madras Agglomeration (*Tamil Nadu*)	2,470,288	42·9
5. Hyderabad Agglomeration (*Andhra Pradesh*)	1,798,910	47·6
6. Ahmedabad Urban Agglomeration (*Gujarat*)	1,746,111	44·8
7. Bangalore Urban Agglomeration (*Mysore*)	1,648,232	36·6
8. Kanpur (*Uttar Pradesh*)	1,273,042	31·1
9. Poona Urban Agglomeration (*Maharashtra*)	1,123,399	52·3

- Some photographs -
illustrations or evidence?
'. . . a bubbling cauldron of
different responses to
population pressure'

Plate 1 In a spice-growing village in the formerly malarious tract of western Mysore, population decrease has been succeeded by increase, but happily there are resources available for local development at no great cost. Here, the landowner is guiding the bucket lifted mainly by the heavy stone at the other end of the lever, and pouring the water down a hollow tree-trunk so that even while the well is being dug, the water is used to irrigate vegetables. His son and a hired labourer are excavating into the bouldery gravels in the valley bottom. At the cost of about £100, the farmer will have the key asset to a very valuable spice garden, though much further work lies ahead. A new well to water a new or remade spice garden is being dug.

Plate 2 The paddy lands have been in effect collectivised, without any legal documents or litigation, but so far as we could find out, simply by common consent, as the only way the people could see of providing a living for everyone, mainly from the village lands. Some families do supplement their cash income by going off to work, usually on nearby coffee plantations. It did not seem to be a response to communist ideology or to the *bhoodan* (land gift) or *gramdan* (village giving its land to itself) movement of the wandering ascetic and holy man Vinobha Bhave. The crop is divided into fifteen equal parts, one for each family. Labour is shared; sick or old people have their work done for them by the able-bodied, but if there are any shirkers they are 'persuaded'.

Plate 3 One traditional means of agricultural intensification, as a response to population pressure, at modest capital investment, is the ox-drawn irrigation from large masonry wells; in Mysore the bucket is self-lift-tipping, emptying into the simple aqueduct and so to the fields of rice, millet, vegetable or sugar cane.

Plate 4 This is a small electric-powered, silk and rayon factory in Tumkur, a smallish town (population 60,000) about 45 miles north-west of Bangalore. We put it in as a complement to the pictures of the large steel plants and the like that we often think of in relation to industrialisation in India. It is modern, well-designed, and by no means lacking in amenities such as a flower-garden. There is some urban pull to even relatively small towns and cities, though rural push factors probably predominate over most of India and may well have been getting much more important in Mysore in the last decade.

Plate 5 Rural push probably activated the vegetable-seller to leave his village, probably in Tamil Nadu (formerly Madras State) and take up this pitch in a respectable working-class area of Bangalore. The tailor has probably been longer a town dweller, perhaps working with a Singer sewing machine from the days of the important British garrison of the colonial phase.

Plate 6 A large village in a dry interior valley near Vellore in Tamil Nadu (formerly Madras State). In South India the Harijans, the formerly outcaste groups, often live in separate hamlets on the edge of the villages. From such hamlets come many of the migrants to the urban slums of Bangalore.

Plate 7 Fish-traps in a minor deltaic distributary near Dacca. Even quite small drainage ditches in rice fields are netted in this way, and fish is an important source of protein in the diet.

Plate 8 The frequently flooded, rich alluvium of the eastern Bengal delta, near Dacca. The new alluvium in the foreground, with paddy fields and fully grown sugar cane, contrasts with the rough pasture and tree cover over laterite on the old alluvium (in background) of an older delta now raised higher by slight earth movements on the edge of the delta.

Plate 9 The narrow canoe-like ferry takes travellers across a deltaic distributary near Dacca. Note the line of houses and orchard trees along the slightly higher levee or spillbank, and the barges and 'country boats' important in transporting rice and jute.

Plate 10 Latrines for some 400 people in a slum area between Calcutta and the Salt Lakes in a deltaic hollow, east of the city. Since provision is so scanty, these are used mainly by women and children, while men and boys use any of the very restricted open spaces around the houses.

Plate 11 A ditch carries black sewage and sullage water within a foot or so of a stand-pipe serving several hundred people in a bad slum on low swampy ground between Calcutta and the Salt Lakes east of the city. The dangers of cholera under these conditions and in the delta, which is one of the great endemic homes of cholera, can be readily imagined.

Plate 12 A relatively prosperous enclave within a slum area east of Calcutta, with rather good houses. The open space is the site of a town dairy, and the shelters are used for milking cows and buffaloes, which yield milk with a high-cream content on especially poor fibrous fodder, but have the disadvantage of less frequent lactations than cows.

Unit 34
Population and Economic Growth

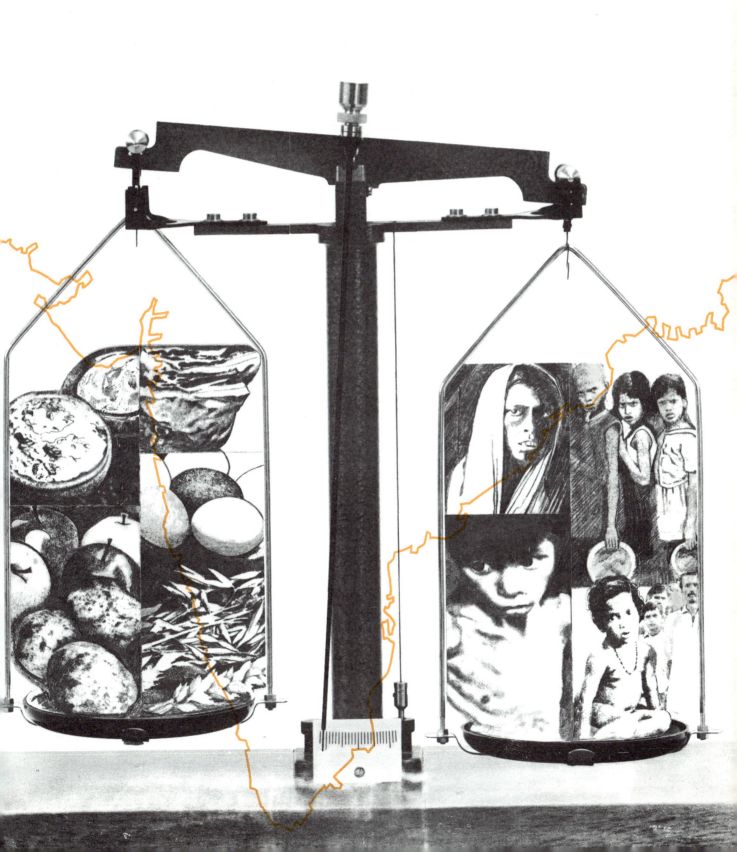

CONTENTS UNIT 34

		PAGE
1	INTRODUCTION	73
2	THE MEASUREMENT OF ECONOMIC DEVELOPMENT	73
3	MALTHUS' THEORY	76
4	ECONOMIC GROWTH AND POPULATION GROWTH	77
	4.1 The Birth Rate	77
	4.2 The Death Rate	78
5	POPULATION GROWTH AND THE FOOD SUPPLY	80
	5.1 The Law of Diminishing Returns	81
	5.2 Food Consumption	85
6	POPULATION GROWTH AND ECONOMIC GROWTH	88
	6.1 The Capital-Output Ratio	89
	6.2 Population Growth as a Stimulus to Economic Growth	91
	6.3 Disguised Unemployment	92
	6.4 Increasing Returns to Scale	93
	6.5 Summary	94
	APPENDIX Mathematical Note	95
	BIBLIOGRAPHY	96
	ACKNOWLEDGEMENTS	96

ECONOMIC IMPLICATIONS OF RAPID POPULATION GROWTH

1 INTRODUCTION

The current population explosion affects most acutely the economically less developed parts of the world. Economists, therefore, interested in the relationship between the growth of population and the development of the economy, have concentrated their attention on analysing this relationship in the developing rather than the developed economies, and the analysis here will also follow this pattern although we will refer to developed economies from time to time for purposes of comparison. One word of warning is necessary before we embark on our analysis. We are not seeking in this unit to provide an adequate treatment of economic development – indeed it would be impossible in the space of one unit – but only of one important factor, namely population growth. So while we will be discussing the relationship between population growth and economic development the student must be warned that the problems of economic growth and development are far more complex than this.

2 THE MEASUREMENT OF ECONOMIC DEVELOPMENT

How do we distinguish between developed and developing countries? When we compare the standards of living of two developed countries we use all sorts of specific measurements such as, for example, the number of motor cars per thousand of population, the percentage of homes owning a washing machine or refrigerator or the percentage of the population in full time higher education. In comparing all countries generally, and particularly the developing ones, the simplest and most relevant measure is to take the total (or gross) output of the country per head of population. This is usually referred to as Gross Domestic Product per head.[1] You will remember from Unit 14 that gross output equals gross income so the income per head of a country measures how much of what it has produced is available for each member of the population. In a very general sense it is a measure of their standard of living although with international comparisons this can be misleading.

Table 1 shows the Gross Domestic Product per head for a number of countries in 1963 and 1966 at current prices. Any international comparison produces problems of statistical interpretation. In this case we are attempting to compare the standards of living of members of different countries by measuring the total amount they have produced. Not all that is produced however, will be consumed, for GDP also includes investment. Some of this will, of course, improve standards of living – such as investment in hospitals, housing, schools, etc. For a more comprehensive treatment of what is included in GDP and how this relates to how much people consume you should refer to Unit 14, pp. 16–17. A further problem

---

[1] For the distinction between GNP and GDP see Unit 14, pp. 13–14.

TABLE 1

GROSS DOMESTIC PRODUCT PER HEAD OF SELECTED COUNTRIES IN 1963 & 1966

	Current U.S. Dollars	
COUNTRY	**1963**	**1966**
U.S.A.	2857	3528
EUROPE (Average)	1170	1470
France	1486	1857
Germany	1420	1750
U.K.	1397	1660
Portugal	317	402
AUSTRALIA	1480	1759
CENTRAL AMERICA (Average)	360	440
SOUTH AMERICA (Average)	320	390
MIDDLE EAST (Average)	280	
Kuwait	4902	4535
Israel	960	1320
Jordan	180	204
ASIA (Average)	150	
Japan	631	919
Ceylon	136	141
India	85	81
AFRICA (Average)	130	
South Africa (including Botswana, Lesotho, etc.)	454	559
Kenya	96	110
Nigeria	71	75
WORLD	600	

Source: U.N. Statistical Year Book, 1968.

is that in some countries certain goods or services are 'free' in economic terms. For example in hot climates no resources need to be made available to produce warmth, spending on clothes may be less, housing provision may not need to be as rigorous and as a result the figure shown in total output for the provision of warmth will be small. In a cold climate a larger proportion of resources will need to be devoted to keeping warm. So while the inhabitants of both countries may obtain the same degree of benefit from warmth one group will have used a great deal more resources to obtain it. Their national output may be at a higher level, but their actual welfare and standard of living will be the same.

International agreement as to what should or should not be included in Gross Domestic Product cannot deal with problems of

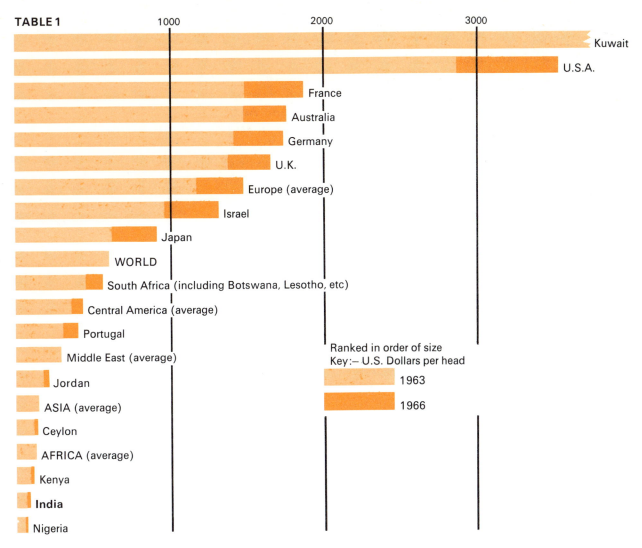

Diagrammatic representation of Table 1

this sort. A further problem is that each country collects its own statistics and some countries are more efficient than others in doing this. Despite these limitations the figures are useful as a guide to international differences in standards of living particularly where the differences are large enough to allow for all the discrepancies mentioned above.

Table 1, for example, shows that the U.S.A. has an income per head nearly five times higher than the world average and that the countries of Western Europe, North America and Australia have a relatively high income per head whilst those in Africa, Asia, Central and South America and the Middle East have a relatively low income per head. The U.S.A. has the highest income per head of any country in the world if we leave aside Kuwait. The reason for ignoring Kuwait is that normally the level of Gross Domestic Product can be used as a measure of the standard of living of a country because it is assumed that the output of a country is produced by its inhabitants and the benefits accrue to its inhabitants. In Kuwait this is not so. A significant proportion of the Gross Domestic Product goes to expatriate oil workers who take most of it out of the country, or to the profits of foreign-owned companies which are also taken out of the country. So while the largest output per head is produced *in* Kuwait only a proportion of it is actually of benefit to the inhabitants *of* Kuwait.[1]

---

[1] See Unit 14, p. 14, footnote 4.

The basic aim of economic development is to raise the income per head of those countries where it is at present relatively low to nearer current European levels. Some would argue that a further aim of development should be to narrow the differential between the European and North American income levels and those of Asia and Africa. In other words it is not sufficient to raise Asian and African levels of income to present European levels in say forty years time if by that time Europe has also increased its income level four or five times. This however, takes us beyond the scope of this unit. We will take the desire for an improved standard of living as given and concentrate on the effect of population growth and population density on the attempt to achieve this desire.

3 MALTHUS' THEORY

It is appropriate to start with the theories of Thomas Malthus for they provide us with a useful conceptual approach to our problem. Malthus published the first edition of his essay on population in 1798. It provoked much controversy at the time and this has rumbled on to the present day. You can read part of Malthus' exposition in his own words in the *Reader* (pp. 643–5) in the passages taken from his *Essay on the Principle of Population*.

Malthus' argument started from the premise that the growth in population was a function of the growth in the food supply. If the supply of food (or more generally the standard of living) increased, the population would also grow. The initial increase in income per head which the increased food supply brought about would fall away as population increased. Moreover, Malthus argued, the increase in population would always tend to be greater than the increase in food production.

Malthus then asked himself the obvious question. If population growth does exceed the growth in the food supply, what happens? His answer was that the limitation of the food supply itself checks population growth. Firstly there were what Malthus called 'positive checks' of which death due to starvation as a result of food shortages, was the most severe. Secondly, there were 'preventive checks', of which the most important, Malthus thought, was a reduction in the birth rate through a delay in the age at marriage. Any attempt to break out of this vicious circle by increasing food production would be self-defeating, because population would grow to meet it, until the subsistence level was reached again, at which level the rate of growth of population would be stabilised for the reasons previously mentioned. The level of subsistence then would determine the size of the population.

It is a pretty depressing picture that Malthus painted and it is easy to see why, as a result of Malthus' theory, economics was referred to as a dismal science. We can summarise its essential propositions as follows:

1 A rising standard of living will increase population.
2 The growth in population will tend to be greater than the growth in food production.
3 The growth in population will only be limited when the standard of living falls to subsistence level.
4 Therefore any attempt to increase the standard of living will be self-defeating because population will grow until the subsistence level is reached again.

Economic historians will be able to say how far Malthus' theory explained conditions in his own day. Our present interest, however, is in seeing how Malthus' view of the population explosion helps to explain the situation in the developing countries today. Studying each of his propositions in turn may throw some light on the problems population growth poses for the economies of the developing countries today. Professor Myint provides some appropriate comments in the extracts from his book quoted in the *Reader* (pp. 645–8).

4 ECONOMIC GROWTH AND POPULATION GROWTH

Malthus' first proposition was that as the standard of living increased population would also increase. Population growth of course is a function of both the birth rate and the death rate. A high birth rate combined with an equally high death rate produces a similar growth in population (either positive, zero or negative) as a low birth rate combined with an equally low death rate.

4.1 The Birth Rate

Taking the birth rate first, Malthus argued that when incomes rose, people could afford to marry earlier. The effect of this would be that more of a woman's childbearing years would be spent in marriage and, therefore, she would be exposed to the risk of having children, and in the societies with which Malthus was familiar would, he asserted, have more children, than if she married later.

There were critics of this approach in Malthus' own day. Nassau Senior (1790–1864) argued that the desire for a higher standard of living was as strong an influence on an individual's behaviour as the desire for procreation. Having tasted a higher standard of living (even in the modest form of more food) a man would attempt to protect this and improve upon it. Thus, a rise in living standards provided an automatic preventive check to the growth of population.

Recently a number of theories have been put forward arguing that economic growth produces a change in attitude to birth control. Note that we are talking about a change in *attitude* for it is argued that ignorance of contraception techniques is not the basic problem although its removal helps once attitudes have changed. Even primitive societies have a knowledge of basic contraception techniques such as that described in the Bible (Genesis 38, 9). The problem is whether people *wish* to practise birth control. Economic growth may cause a change of attitude in a number of ways. It may involve a movement from a rural to an urban environment bringing with it a weakening of religious ties that may have associated with attitudes opposing birth control. The political and industrial emancipation of women has also led to their awareness of other functions in life besides child-bearing and rearing.

Professor Blaug (1968, p. 78) argues that these socio-economic factors with regard to having children, can be formalised into a *cost-benefit* analysis. A cost-benefit analysis weighs up all the relevant costs and all the relevant benefits of a particular action and compares them, to see whether the outcome is a net cost or a net benefit. The higher the net benefit the greater is the chance of the action being undertaken. In this particular case Professor Blaug argues that in developed countries the costs to parents of having children have risen while the benefits have been reduced so that the net benefit of having children is now much lower than previously. Costs have been increased through the reduced ability of the mother to work; the increase in the school-leaving age, which postpones the child's contribution to household finances; and the expense of housing, which means that large families in urban populations are often the victims of over-crowding. Whereas in agricultural units, based on the family, children can contribute to the running of the farm from quite an early age, in an industrialised economy, child labour in factories is likely to be prohibited. Added to this, the weakening of family ties sometimes associated with the process of industrialisation reduces the returns from children in the form of old-age security, pride in their achievement and obedience to parental will.

It is an interesting theory and no doubt we can all review our own attitudes in the light of it. We do not have to follow it in all its details, however, to accept that, historically, a higher standard of living has produced a more permissive attitude to contraception and a reduction in the birth rate.

4.2 The Death Rate

Turning to the death rate, it is generally agreed that economic development can produce a reduction in the rate through three sets of factors. Firstly, starvation is more adequately coped with either through a more efficient production of food, or through a more efficient food distribution system, the latter stemming from improvements in communications, and more liberal trade policies leading to surplus food in one area being more easily transported to other, more needy, areas. It is estimated that this can reduce the death rate by as much as one per cent per annum. The populations of India and some African countries in fact rose at an annual rate of one per cent in the first half of this century when slightly lower death rates, caused at least partly by these factors, coincided with high birth rates. And a one per cent growth rate in India is not an insignificant amount. At present levels of population it means an extra five to six million people per annum. The death rate has fallen further in the last twenty years as these countries have come under the influence of two other factors that affect the death rate.

The first of these is the adoption of public health measures which control both epidemics and such endemic diseases as typhoid, malaria and smallpox, etc. These measures may also reduce the death rate by one per cent per annum so that countries which have adopted them and improved their food distribution, without reducing their birth rate, can expect their population to grow at two per cent per annum, or in other words, to double every thirty-five years. The average rate of population growth in the developing countries during the 1950s was slightly above this rate and figures for the 1960s indicate that the rate has risen to about two and a half per cent per annum.

The second factor is the extension of individual medical facilities to a large proportion of the population. This too can reduce the death rate by one per cent per annum. So a country which has adopted all three sets of measures without, at the same time, reducing the birth rate, will have a population growing at a rate of three per cent per annum.

Economic development therefore can reduce the death rate by as much as three per cent per annum and with no fall in birth rates this would produce a doubling of population in under twenty-five years. The increase in the food supply – which was what Malthus meant by an increase in living standards – is then today not the only cause of increased population growth. The major cause is the increase in standards of medical care which has the effect of lowering the death rate. Improvements in the food supply operate only at the lowest levels of subsistence, and at these levels it will cause population to increase by only one per cent per annum, and this normally through a reduction in the death rate rather than an increase in the birth rate as Malthus postulated. If a one per cent rise in population were all there were to cope with, food supply might keep up with it for a very long time.

Malthusians can argue, however, that even if he did not foresee the modern developments which have changed the factors affecting population growth, since his own day, the overall proposition remains true, that a rise in the standard of living increases the rate of growth of population. We have shown that today the mechanism is through a reduction in the death rate rather than an increase in the birth rate, but the end result is still the same.

However Malthus is correct only in a limited sense. We must ask why the present developed countries did not suffer the same problems during the same stage of their development. This is a complex question, but a general answer is that the effects were much more gradual. These countries adopted new techniques of food production and new medical methods only slowly, so that the reduction in the death rate was a gradual one. Later the emancipation of women and the effects of the industrial revolution produced a reduction in the birth rate so that both it and the death rate fell gradually with the result that the rate of the growth of population proceeded relatively slowly.

Having produced these developments Western countries are now exporting them wholesale to the developing countries where their impact is much greater. In Ceylon for example, malaria was wiped out in seven years with a consequent fall in the death rate of one per cent per annum. In the U.K. a similar fall in the rate took seventy years.

The basic problem of the developing countries is that we have 'westernised' them with regard to the death rate but not with regard to the birth rate. At present they have high birth rates characteristic of agrarian economies and low death rates characteristic of industrialised economies. Medical science has been applied to the prevention of death but not birth.

We have seen that as economic development proceeds the birth rate might be expected to fall so that the present problem could solve itself in fifty or more years time. The Malthusian argument may then apply only over a limited time-period. In the long run his proposition that a higher standard of living leads to a faster population growth does not seem valid.

There is no room for complacency, however, for a number of reasons. Firstly we cannot just ignore fifty or more years and wait for the birth rate to fall. Also there is no automatic reason why the developing countries should follow the developed countries' example. Furthermore, the high growth in population may so inhibit the ability to develop the economy, that the stage where birth rates fall is never reached. This leads on to a discussion of Malthus' next point, namely that the growth in population will tend to outstrip the growth in the food supply, for if this is true – or even approximately true – it means that the developing countries will have to use so many of their resources simply to provide food, that there will be few resources available to concentrate on improving standards of living. Like the Red Queen of *Alice in Wonderland*, 'they will have to run faster and faster in order to stand still'.

TEST 1

5 **POPULATION GROWTH AND THE FOOD SUPPLY**

In arguing that the increase in population tends to outstrip the increase in the food supply, Malthus was starting from a position in which people already lived at subsistence level, so that taking the density of the population, measured say by food resources or cultivable land per person, as already at its maximum level, Malthus could produce a direct link between food supply and population growth.

In examining conditions today we cannot make this assumption, for if density is not at the highest possible level, we can allow for population growth to exceed the growth of the food supply to a limited extent. So studying the problem now we have to look at both the density and growth of population.

Taking density of population first we will use two measures. The first looks at density from the point of view of food resources, by defining it as the amount of agricultural area or cultivable land per person. Looking at the problem in a world context we can see that the world as a whole is not over-populated from a food supply point of view. It is estimated that the world's total area of cultivable land is more than 15,000 million acres and this has to support about 3,700 million people so that there are over four acres per person. The minimum acceptable amount of cultivable land that is needed will depend on our techniques of food production and our pattern of consumption. Taking the most productive methods of cultivation and a Western standard of consumption Professor Colin Clark (1967) has estimated that the minimum area per person could be about 1.3 acres and therefore the existing area of land could support 12,000 million people. So the world's population would have to nearly quadruple before a world shortage of food became apparent. There is some controversy over this estimate. Others have argued that even if all the cultivable land not now cultivated were opened up so that the maximum of 15,000 million acres was reached, the result would only be sufficient to raise nutrition standards of today's population to the European level, and there would be no surplus to cater for a further growth of population. The crucial argument is however whether the most productive methods of cultivation can be applied in all areas of the world.

A further problem is that Clark's analysis is about the *potential* world food production capacity. There is no guarantee that resources will be put to food production even if people are starving, particularly if the resources and the people are in different countries. We will deal with this point later.

Finally, while we may be able to provide physically for a growth in population by having enough land on which to increase our food supply, the more of our resources we have to devote to food production, the less we can provide for the other wants of a developed economy. We will expand on this point later too.

But even if Clark's analysis is correct in the world context there may be problems in specific areas of the world. Professor Myint gives figures (*Reader*, p. 646) for the agricultural area per person of different continents. This shows Asia with 1.5 acres, Latin America 6.9 acres and Africa with 10.6 acres. The significance of these figures for the supply of food depends on the productivity of the land and the state of technology. Europe has roughly the same number of acres per person as Asia, but the level of technology and industrialisation enables it to provide for some of its food needs through the exchange of manufactured goods exports for food imports. The developing countries will themselves have different levels of technology, but even so the figures indicate that Asia has a more pressing food supply problem than Latin America and most of Africa. The latter continents may be able to afford a high population growth rate for some time without formidable problems of food supply.

We have concentrated on the ability to survive in the context of having enough food. There is a further condition for survival and this is having enough *space*. The total land area of the globe including desert, ice and mountain is about fifty-seven million square miles or 32,448 million acres. If we allot each person only one square yard for standing room and world population grows at two per cent per annum we shall have used up all our space in about 550 years time. By then of course we may be living on another planet, but this calculation serves to highlight the pressure of population growth on the supply of land.

Once again however, if we turn to the situation in specific areas of the world the problem is less remote and far more pressing than it appears when the world as a whole is looked at. This brings us to our second measure of density, namely the number of people per square kilometre of area. The *United Nations Statistical Year Book* for 1968 shows that in the previous year, India had 156 people per square kilometre, Ghana 34, Kenya 17, Brazil 10 and Argentina 8.

It seems, therefore, that in India and other parts of Asia, both from the point of view of food supply and land space, we may have a population density situation akin to that from which Malthus started. We now have to ask whether it is likely that population growth will exceed the growth of the food supply. As far as history is concerned Malthus appears to have been wrong, at least, if one looks at the world as a whole, during the course of the nineteenth century. Estimates of the half-century before the First World War indicate that the world food supply grew by two per cent per annum while world population grew by 0.7 per cent per annum. We have already seen why population grew at a lower rate than Malthus expected. We now have to understand why food supply grew at a faster rate than Malthus postulated. In order to understand this we have to investigate the principle on which Malthus based his argument about the growth of the food supply – a principle which became known as the *Law of Diminishing Returns*.[1]

5.1 The Law of Diminishing Returns

This law was first explained in Unit 11, pp. 39–41. It demonstrates what is likely to occur when successive units of a variable factor of

---

[1] Although Malthus utilised the ideas inherent in the law of diminishing returns, the law itself was not formulated until some years after the first edition of his *Essay*.

production (e.g. labour) are combined with a fixed quantity of other factors of production (e.g. land and capital). At first each successive unit of the variable factor is likely to produce a higher return than a previous unit as the fixed factors are used more effectively. There comes a point, however, when each successive unit begins to produce less than a previous unit, and, as more and more units of the variable factor are combined with the fixed factors, the increase in output becomes less and less until there is probably a negative effect on output.

The idea is illustrated by the following example. Assuming a farmer has a limited number of acres which he has to farm and a fixed amount of capital equipment (e.g. a few ploughs, spades, etc.), then if he employs just one man, he finds the fellow has to work (say) 100 hours a week to cover the whole land. He can only use one plough, leaving the rest idle, and he is so tired that the land is not farmed very well. It will certainly pay the farmer to employ another chap who can use the other plough, share the burden and probably produce a more than proportionate increase in output. A third and fourth man may enable some further specialisation and division of labour to take place, thus producing a more than proportionate increase in output again. With the amount of land and capital fixed, however, there soon comes a limit to the number of extra men he can take on. They eventually have to start sharing the ploughs and get in each other's way on the land. The increases in output resulting from taking on more and more people become smaller and smaller until eventually there are so many surplus workers getting in each other's way that extra workers probably reduce output rather than increase it. This is not because the extra workers are any less efficient. The physical situation simply prevents them from doing their job.

The law itself does not enable us to say when we should stop employing extra men for we need to know the cost of each extra man before such a decision can be made, and this part of the analysis more properly belongs to the theory of the firm. We are interested here in establishing that eventually diminishing returns to a variable factor do set in when increasing units of it are combined with fixed factors. This idea is illustrated graphically below.

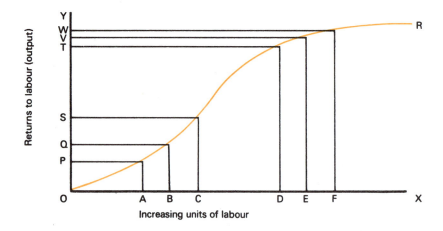

Figure 34.1

The X axis measures the increasing units of labour used, while the Y axis measures the returns (or output) as more units are used. The curve OR is in two parts. In the early stages, with just a few units used, an increase in labour produces a more than proportionate return in output. For example an increase in labour from OB to OC produces an increase in output from OQ to OS. It is noticeable that the increase in labour BC, which is the same magnitude as the increase AB, produces a much larger increase in output (QS as opposed to PQ). This situation is known as one of *increasing returns*. Eventually, however, we move to a situation further along the curve where an increase in labour EF of similar magnitude to the previous increase DE produces less of an increase in output than the previous unit (VW as opposed to TV). *Diminishing returns* have set in. The law states that eventually this must occur.

Malthus applied the principle to the problem of world food supply. He argued that the world supply of land was fixed, so that as population increased the increasing amount of labour used on the land would produce diminishing returns and the supply of food would be less and less. We can amend Figure 34.1 to show Malthus' application.

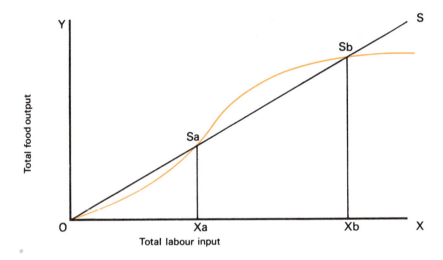

Figure 34.2

In Figure 34.2 the Y axis measures total food output and the X axis measures total labour input. The curve OR is similar to the OR curve in Figure 34.1, An additional line, OS, has been drawn on the graph passing through the axis. This is known as the subsistence line, as it measures the total amount of food needed to maintain the population at subsistence level, at each level of population. It is based on the principle that an increasing level of labour (or population) requires a proportionate increase in the food supply. For example suppose the subsistence level is five tons of food per person per year. One million people will require five million tons of food for subsistence; two million people will require ten million tons, three million people will require fifteen million tons and so on. The OS line measures the subsistence level of food requirements for each level of population. The OR line measures the total food output produced by each level of population. Therefore, Figure 34.2 enables us to compare the difference between food production and minimum food consumption at each level of population.

According to Figure 34.2, population cannot be below the level Xa. At any population level between O and Xa the food supply (as measured by OR) is below the minimum level required (as measured by OS). As a result some people will die. As population falls subsistence requirements will fall, but so will food production. The inevitable result is that population will decline to zero.

83

So, in the situation shown in Figure 34.2 the minimum level of population is Xa corresponding to the minimum subsistence level Sa. As population grows beyond Xa food production grows faster than subsistence. At any population level between Xa and Xb population can enjoy food consumption above its subsistence requirements – as shown by the arc between Sa and Sb. Malthus argued, however, that as the standard of living improved this would lead to an increase in the level of population. Eventually population level Xb is reached at which food consumption is at subsistence level Sb. Any attempt to increase population above Xb would fail because the minimum level of subsistence is above the total food supply and so population would fall back to Xb. Moreover population would not be reduced below Xb because, Malthus argued, the improvement in the standard of living would eventually lead to a population increase back to Xb. So population would be stabilised at Xb which would be the minimum subsistence level of food consumption.

The law of diminishing returns makes three assumptions. These are that technological progress is stationary and that both capital and land are fixed. Each of these assumptions will now be discussed.

The most important assumption is that technology does not change. Malthus accepted that technological progress might have some effect on increasing the productivity of land, but argued that this effect could not overcome the declining productivity brought about by diminishing returns.

The effect of technological progress is that each unit of labour produces more output than before. In terms of the OR curve in Figures 34.1 and 34.2 this curve shifts upwards as shown in Figure 34.3 below.

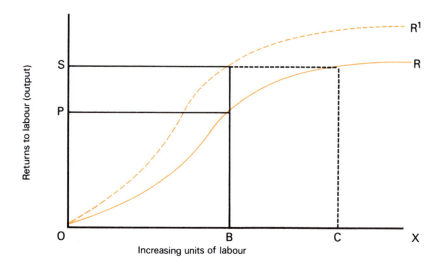

Figure 34.3

The graph shows that the result of technological progress is that the OR curve is raised to a new curve OR^1. With the new curve the same amount of labour OB will now produce OS of output instead of OP as with the old curve. If technological progress was stationary and OS output was required the amount of labour needed would have been OC as is shown by the dotted line in Figure 34.3.

Now if the subsistence line is drawn on the graph as was done in Figure 34.2 the effect of changing technological progress on Malthus' argument can be seen. This is shown in Figure 34.4.

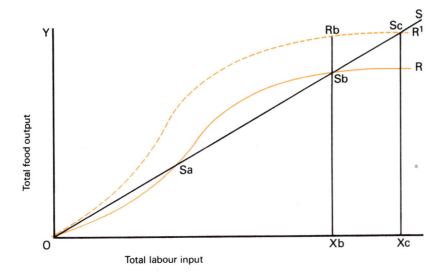

Figure 34.4

The effect of technological progress is to shift the OR curve to OR¹ so that food supply at Rb is above the subsistence level Sb. In fact with technological progress population can increase to Xc before subsistence level Sc is reached. The main reason why Malthus' predictions have been falsified is that technological progress has improved food productivity so that the OR curve has been pushed higher and higher and allowed population to grow without ever reaching subsistence level. The increasing use of fertilisers for example has certainly had a beneficial effect on food production. Sir John Russell (1954, p. 65) has calculated that the use of one ton of nitrogen fertiliser together with the necessary phosphate and potash gives an average of ten additional tons of starch equivalent, sufficient to feed forty persons a year.

A second reason why history proved Malthus wrong is that a second assumption underlying the law of diminishing returns – that the supply of land is fixed – has not so far been fulfilled. Malthus underestimated the amounts of new land that might be brought into cultivation. We have already seen that, taking the world as a whole, the pessimistic estimate is that we can just manage to feed the present population of the world while the optimistic estimate is that population can afford to quadruple, if new lands are brought into cultivation. In addition there is always the possibility that further technical progress will enable us to improve our methods of cultivation.

Finally, the law of diminishing returns assumes capital to be fixed. But, if a larger amount of physical capital is used then more output per unit of labour is likely to be produced. And in most economies the capital/labour ratio has increased as development has proceeded.

The law of diminishing returns therefore, is relevant to a static situation at a given point of time. It takes no account of changes in technology, land, or capital. Malthus' use of it led him to underestimate the potential increase in food supply just as his theories of population growth led him to overestimate the likely demand for food. The law, is however, useful as a warning of how food subsistence levels might be reached if food production cannot be increased through increased technology, capital or land.

5.2 Food Consumption

It seems therefore that Malthus' predictions as to the rate of population growth and the rate of growth of the food supply have not been accurate when applied to the world as a whole. We have seen, however, that in certain areas of the world, populations are approaching Malthusian growth rates even if the mechanism is different from that put forward by Malthus. Might it not be the case that while there is no overall world food shortage, problems will occur in these high population growth areas? The United Nations (1968) has published a report which estimates that over a third of the population in developing countries has an inadequate protein-calorie balance.

It is, however, very difficult to decide upon the minimum level of food required. It depends on the amount of work undertaken, the climate and the physical characteristics of the people involved. Calories are needed for energy, and protein for the maintenance of bodily organs and muscles. Calories can be seen as the quantity of food required and proteins as the quality. A minimum number of different proteins are needed to maintain a healthy body but an adequate number of calories is the main requirement in a subsistence diet.

The Food and Agriculture Organisation of the United Nations has calculated minimum calorie requirements for a number of countries. These have caused much controversy mainly because, as we have explained, there are so many different factors to take into account. It is generally accepted, however, that a minimum subsistence diet should contain more than 2,000 calories per day. The table below shows the average calorie consumption per person per day for a number of countries in the period 1965–67.

TABLE 2

Calorie Consumption Per Person Per Day – 1965, 1966 or 1967

Country		Calorie Consumption
India	1965/66	1810
Iran	1966	1890
Sudan	1966	1940
Afghanistan	1966	1950
Ceylon	1966	2180
Pakistan	1965/66	2290
Mauritius	1966	2370
France	1966/67	3150
U.S.A.	1967	3200
U.K.	1966/67	3220
Denmark	1966/67	3300

Source: U.N. Statistical Year Book 1968 – Tables 167/168.

The table shows that while the developed countries consume in excess of 3,000 calories per person per day, a number of poorer countries, notably India, are well below a minimum calorie consumption, while others such as Ceylon and Pakistan are not far

TABLE 2

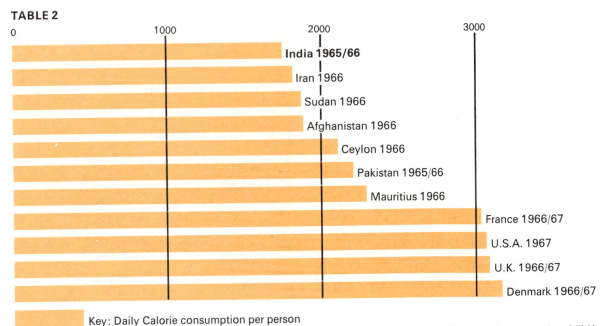

Key: Daily Calorie consumption per person

Diagrammatic representation of Table 2

above the minimum. The implication of these figures is that many people in these countries live very close to a starvation diet and are unable to work as hard as they might given an adequate calorie consumption. In these countries a food supply problem does exist and as the United Nations has pointed out, Malthus' argument that population growth will outgrow food supplies could well be justified.

The position therefore seems to be that *potentially* there is enough capacity in the world to provide an adequate food supply in the foreseeable future, but in reality some countries are eating more than the minimum (and probably more than is desirable) whereas others are finding it difficult to achieve the minimum.

Few countries are self-sufficient in that they can provide *all* their own food needs. As in all economic activity, countries specialise in what they are best able to produce and exchange these goods through international trade for goods which other countries produce. Some countries concentrate on certain kinds of food production, exchanging food for industrial products, while others do the opposite. As far as food is concerned the table below indicates the amount of food that certain countries produce for themselves.

TABLE 3

Domestic Production as a Percentage of the Total Supply of Food in Selected Countries

Country	Wheat & Rye	Rice	Potatoes	Sugar	Meat
Australia	536%	319%	102%	353%	145%
India	56%	97%	100%	106%	100%
U.K.	46%	—	95%	37%	65%
U.S.A.	230%	294%	106%	50%	100%

Source: United Nations Statistical Year Book, 1968.

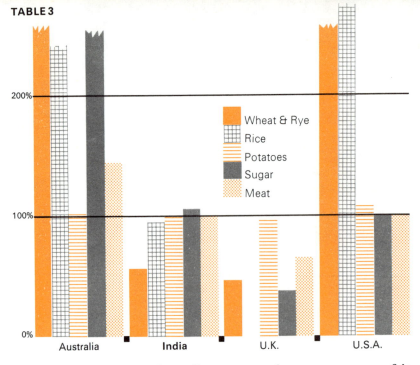

TABLE 3

Diagrammatic representation of Table 3

The figures show that Australia exports a large percentage of its food production while India has very little surplus and in fact has to import nearly half of its wheat and rye supplies. The United Kingdom produces much less of its own food supplies than India but the crucial difference is that the U.K., having a developed economy, produces many other goods which it can exchange for imported food, while India does not have the resources to provide many manufactured goods for the world market.

The problem, therefore, is not that the world cannot produce enough food but that the countries whose need for food is greatest:

(a) cannot produce enough themselves; or
(b) cannot produce enough non-food products to exchange for imported food; or
(c) devote so many of their resources to providing food, or goods to exchange for food, that they have very few resources left to produce the other goods and services they require.

It is clear from this that the question of an adequate supply of food cannot be studied in isolation from the supply of other goods. For a country whose economy is developing and whose output is growing finds it can supply more of its own food or else produce more goods which can be exchanged for imported food. We must extend our analysis to look at the effects of population growth on the development of an individual economy.

TEST 2

6 POPULATION GROWTH AND ECONOMIC GROWTH

Economic growth involves the transition from a subsistence (or primitive) agricultural economy to an industrialised one and different countries are at various stages of this transition. Among the factors normally required to facilitate this process are a stable political system, an efficient administration, an infrastructure of roads, railways, electricity, hospitals, schools, etc., a high level of capital investment and a literate and increasingly educated population. Much controversy exists over which factors ought to be given priority, but it is generally agreed that a high level of capital investment is of vital importance. The mechanism by which investment produces growth is a complex one, but it is mainly the incorporation of technological progress in capital equipment and the substitution of capital for labour, which enables goods to be produced more efficiently.

6.1 The Capital-Output Ratio

The effect of capital on output can be stated in terms of what is called a capital-output ratio. A marginal capital-output ratio of four means that we have to devote four per cent of our national income (i.e. our total resources) to capital investment in order to raise output by one per cent. It's called marginal because it's the *extra* capital needed to produce some extra output. A ratio of five similarly means that we have to devote five per cent of our current output to investment to achieve a growth of one per cent. The smaller the marginal capital-output ratio (i.e. the higher the capital productivity) the better are the chances of growth, for a smaller percentage of the country's resources need then be devoted to investment in order to achieve any given growth rate.

The concept as explained above seems a marvellously elementary way of showing how economic growth occurs. The student should not, however, be deluded into thinking that all he has to do is find the marginal capital-output ratio for any country, apply the simple arithmetical formula and thereby show what it has to do in order to achieve any given growth rate. We have already explained that many other factors are involved in economic development and some economists have objected to the use of the marginal capital-output ratio itself.

A major problem is that it is an *aggregate* marginal capital-output ratio for the whole economy, involving an averaging out of the different marginal capital-output ratios for different sectors of the economy. It is generally accepted, for example, that agriculture has a low marginal capital-output ratio in that the introduction of quite elementary capital equipment (e.g. a plough) can increase output substantially. The building of railways and roads on the other hand necessitates a high level of investment for any increase in output to occur at all. The various manufacturing industries will also have different marginal capital-output ratios.

A particular country's overall ratio will depend on what aspect of economic development it is concentrating on, or more relevantly, the aspects of development it concentrates on will depend on the availability of capital resources. A country with scarce capital might decide to concentrate on improving agricultural productivity, through buying agricultural equipment, rather than building a road or railway. The problem is a complex one and our use of an overall marginal capital-output ratio should not make the student forget that a great deal of complex interaction in the economy lies behind the overall ratio. Also he should not take the ratio as fixed, for a basic aim of all economies is to improve their capital productivity and thus lower their marginal capital-output ratios.

Despite these difficulties the marginal capital-output ratio is a useful concept in explaining the effects of population growth. Assume for example that a developing economy has an aggregate marginal capital-output ratio of four to one determined by the particular sectors of the economy on which it is concentrating its capital investment. (This in fact is about the average for the marginal capital-output ratios of developed economies.) The ratio means that if it wishes to grow at two per cent per annum it must devote eight per cent of its annual output to investment; a three per cent growth rate implies devoting twelve per cent of its output to investment and so on.

But if growth is to mean an increase in the output available for each member of the population it must mean an increase in *output per head*. Thus if population is growing by one per cent, a three per cent overall increase in output means only a two per cent increase in output per head. You will notice that we have *subtracted* the growth in population from the growth in output to obtain the growth in output per head.[1]

The importance of population growth is now clear. Having studied the relationship between investment and output we can see that if a country wishes to grow at the modest rate of two per cent per annum with a marginal capital-output ratio of four to one it must devote eight per cent of its output to investment. If its population is growing at one per cent per annum then a two per cent increase in output per head requires a three per cent overall increase in output indicating that twelve per cent of current output must be devoted to investment. But if population is growing by three per cent, then a two per cent increase in output per head implies a five per cent overall increase in output, indicating that twenty per cent of resources must be devoted to investment. The faster the growth in population the larger must be the proportion of resources devoted to investment in order to achieve any given growth rate.

Population growth produces a further problem, however, for not only does it necessitate a higher level of investment, but it also makes that higher level more difficult to achieve. If the economy is in equilibrium an increase in investment requires a corresponding increase in saving (defined as the difference between total income and consumption). If a country needs to devote twenty per cent of its current output to investment in order to achieve a two per cent increase in output per head (i.e. assuming a three per cent increase in population and a marginal capital-output ratio of four to one) then it must save twenty per cent of its total income each year.

It is difficult to obtain up-to-date marginal capital-output ratios for developing countries. The third Indian five year plan assumed an overall ratio of 2.2 per cent, indicating clearly that much of the capital would be invested in agriculture and small industries. With Indian population growing at 2.5 per cent per annum in the first half of the 1960s, and a marginal capital-output ratio of 2.2 per cent, capital investment, and therefore saving, would have to take up 5.5 per cent of national income just to maintain the existing level of income per head. It is difficult to get figures for exactly the same years as the third plan, but between 1963 and 1965 India in fact

---

[1] Strictly speaking we should have *divided* population growth into output growth to obtain output per head growth. However, when small percentages are involved the difference in the answers from these two methods is very small and we have kept to the simpler method for purposes of exposition because it gives us answers in whole numbers. Those students not understanding the difference in the two methods should read the mathematical note at the end of the unit. To reiterate the point, the increase in population is subtracted from the increase in output to achieve an increase in output per head.

saved eleven per cent of its national income while output per head hardly rose at all indicating that the marginal capital-output ratio was higher than was planned for. The average savings ratio in all developing countries in 1965 was fourteen per cent compared with twenty-two per cent in the developed countries.

The reason the developing countries did not save more is that they could not afford to. For the nearer you are to a subsistence economy the less you have available for saving. In fact population growth has a doubly negative effect on saving. Firstly, it necessitates more of national income being devoted to investment and secondly by pre-empting more income for food consumption it prevents the community achieving savings levels, through which these investment rates can be achieved. Indeed India and other developing countries have found it necessary to bridge their savings and investment gaps by the import of capital. In effect the savings of the developed economies have been used to provide investment in developing economies so that they may grow faster and eventually provide their own higher savings ratio.

6.2 **Population Growth as a Stimulus to Economic Growth**

Before leaving the study of the relationship between population growth, capital investment and economic growth, attention must be drawn to other points of view, and particularly the contrasting argument that population pressure is a positive encouragement to economic development.

Economists who take this line admit that the process of economic development involves a great deal of sacrifice. Labour has to be taken off food production and put into producing agricultural implements, transport and irrigation facilities. A country already hard-pressed to feed its population has to sacrifice some present food consumption in order to provide capital equipment to increase future output. A basic economic problem of any society – how to allocate its resources between consumption and investment – is even more acute in developing countries where the amount to be saved is larger and the means to save smaller. There is also the social disruption which accompanies a change in the pace and form of economic activity.

So far there is little difference between this argument and that explained earlier, for both accept that developing countries with large populations need to save more and also find it correspondingly more difficult to do so. Professors Clark (1967) and Hirschman (1958) have argued, however, that given the large sacrifices that need to be made, no country will undertake such a programme unless it is forced to. It is population pressure making life miserable that forces a country to make the changes and sacrifices necessary to enable it to climb out of its misery. Without the pressure of population producing near-starvation and miserable living conditions, a country might be content to drift along just above subsistence level, preferring to keep its settled way of life and not wishing to undergo the economic and social upheaval that accompanies economic growth. This argument still accepts that a higher rate of population growth calls for a higher rate of investment for every given rate of output growth. But, it is argued, a country is only moved to attempt to achieve a higher output growth because of the pressure of population growth.

These contrasting arguments are a good example of how small

differences in emphasis in economics can lead to completely opposite policy conclusions. Both points of view accept the capital-output ratio argument outlined previously. By arguing, however, that population pressure is the main spur to the desire to achieve economic growth, even though it makes growth harder to achieve, the Clark-Hirschman argument comes out in favour of *stimulating* population growth in low density areas. On the other hand, our earlier argument clearly led to the conclusion that population growth should be slowed down.

6.3 Disguised Unemployment

It has been argued, further, that while population *growing* at a fast rate may necessitate a higher level of investment, a large population *size* may help to speed the process of industrialisation. This argument is explained in some detail in the extract in the *Reader* from Professor Lewis's *Theory of Economic Growth* and it refers to a situation known as 'disguised unemployment'.

This is said to exist in developing countries with large populations where, because of inadequate employment opportunities, surplus labour tends to gather in existing occupations. Usually this is in agriculture where whole families live off an area of land that could be cultivated quite adequately by one or two members. It also occurs in other occupations such as petty trading where two or three people look after a stall which one could look after quite adequately, or in domestic service where a whole family may be taken in, even though the mother or father could do the work on their own. It is called 'disguised unemployment' because this surplus labour could be withdrawn altogether, without there being any fall in output. This surplus labour can be of use in economic development, for it can be taken off the land where its absence will lead to no decline in agricultural output and put to work in the construction of productive capital goods such as roads, or schools, or in manufacturing industry. The existence of a large population in a developing country may, therefore, provide a pool of surplus labour which can be allocated to other activities without reducing the agricultural output needed to feed the population. Even if there is some reduction in agricultural output this is likely to be more than offset by the extra output produced elsewhere.

This argument was very popular during the 1950s when Lewis wrote his book, but it has received much critical attention since then. Its beauty lies in the fact that it seems to offer something for nothing, in that non-food output can be increased without diminishing agricultural output.

This is now disputed. In reality 'disguised unemployment' does not occur by, for example, two people working eight hours a day and two others sitting about idly. The four of them work four hours a day or stretch their work habits over eight hours so that only four hours effective work is done. Now if we take two people off the land as being surplus and put them into industry, we have to persuade the other two to put in a full eight-hour day, if agricultural output is not to fall. They will probably not be used to this and in any case will require some economic incentive to raise their work-rate. They will probably wish to acquire manufactured consumer goods with their food surpluses, and ideally these would be provided by the workers who have been transferred to industry. Setting up a simple model, we would have changed from a situation where all the people worked in agriculture, supplying all their own food needs, but consuming little else, to a situation where half worked twice as hard in agriculture producing the same total output and exchanging this for surplus consumer goods produced by the other half that had been transferred into industry.

Two factors distort this rather neat analysis. Firstly, it is in the nature of economic development that consumer goods are not the first priority in development. Capital goods such as roads, hospitals and irrigation works are usually the first necessity. The need to provide consumer goods as incentives produces economic and social strains which may not be easy to overcome. Secondly, the changing employment pattern will probably increase the demand for food. Both the workers left on the land and the workers transferred to the new employment will be working much harder than before and their food requirements and consumption will rise accordingly. The workers left on the land will thus have to produce even more than *all* the workers were producing before the transfer, either by working harder or by using more advanced capital equipment, better fertilisers, etc. This is an extra cost of transferring labour from agriculture to industry. Further costs are also incurred. The transfer from agriculture to industry probably involves a change from a rural to an urban environment, involving the provision of extra housing and communal facilities. Thus the creation of employment to absorb 'disguised unemployment' can be justified only if its extra output in the new occupations is large enough to cover the extra consumption which is generated. In many cases it will be and a net benefit to the economy accrues from transferring workers from agriculture to industry. The size of this net benefit, however, is not as large as was earlier believed. We are now much more aware of the extra costs and other limitations involved in taking advantage of a large population in a developing country.

Furthermore, even if there is a benefit in using the surplus labour in agriculture to build up the industrial sector, it doesn't automatically mean that this will occur. In fact many of the industrial projects in the developing countries use very little labour, concentrating instead on methods of production that use a great deal of capital rather than labour. The reasons for this are complex, but a major factor is that outside loans and grants can be obtained more readily for the purchase of capital equipment than for the payment of more labour. A developing country with scarce financial resources is obviously attracted by the idea of having someone else pay for its capital equipment. So while the employment situation might bias a country into using methods of production which use a great deal of labour (i.e. labour-intensive), the financial incentives bias them into using methods of production that use a great deal of capital (i.e. capital-intensive).

6.4 Increasing Returns to Scale

Once an economy is on the road to economic development a large and growing population may be beneficial. This is because many important industries show increasing returns to scale (Unit 11, pp. 39–41), i.e. the larger the scale of production the more economical it becomes, because costs per unit of output fall. This applies particularly to the public utilities such as transport, electricity, gas and water. These show marked economies as population grows more dense since their facilities are more fully utilised, with very little increase in costs. In some countries an increase in the size of the population is required to enable these facilities to be provided by industries of the optimum size.

A number of manufacturing industries also show increasing returns to scale, particularly those requiring large capital investments such as steel production. A country with a large population is in a better position to set up these large-scale industries requiring large labour forces and in some cases a large home market, than a country with a small population. However, large units are not always the most efficient means of production where smaller units are technically possible, but we must leave this aspect of industrial structure for a different course. Where large-scale production is the only feasible method, a large and growing population facilitates production at cheaper cost.

6.5 **Summary**

A summary view of the effects of population growth on economic growth is that a fast-growing population calls for a faster rate of economic growth while at the same time making that rate more difficult to achieve. However, in certain cases it can facilitate faster growth through providing surplus labour to be transferred from agriculture to industry although the benefits are not as large as was once thought. Once economic development has begun, a large and growing population will facilitate the establishment of large-scale production industries.

TEST 3

APPENDIX

I
MATHEMATICAL NOTE

Output and Output per Head

It was stated in the section on the capital-output ratio (6.1) that the growth in output per head can be obtained either by *dividing* output growth by population growth or *subtracting* population growth from output growth. The results obtained from these two methods are not very different and the latter method was used because it was simpler. This note is intended to illustrate the similarity in the results obtained from these two methods.

Example 1

    The growth in output is   5% i.e. 1.05
    The growth in population is 2% i.e. 1.02

If we use the first method and *divide* output growth by population growth the result is:

$$1.02 \overline{)1.05} = 1.0294$$

```
              1.0294
       ┌─────────────
  1.02 │ 1.05
         1.02
         ─────
          .0300
          .0204
          ─────
            960
            918
           ────
            420
            408
           ────
             12
```

If you work through the division yourself you will see that the answer is 1.0294 or in other words *2.94 per cent*.

If we use the second method and *subtract* population growth from output growth the result is:

$$\begin{array}{r} 1.05 \\ -\,1.02 \\ \hline =\ .03 \end{array}$$ or in other words *3 per cent*.

Example 2

    The growth in output is   10% i.e. 1.10
    The growth in population is 5% i.e. 1.05

If we use the first method and *divide* output growth by population growth the result is:

```
              1.0476
       ┌─────────────
  1.05 │ 1.10
         1.05
         ─────
          0500
           420
          ────
           800
           735
          ────
           650
           630
          ────
            20
```
(cont.)

The answer is 1.0476 or *4.76 per cent*.

If we use the second method and *substract* population growth from output growth the result is:

$$\begin{array}{r} 1.10 \\ -\,1.05 \\ \hline =\ .05 \end{array}$$ or *5 per cent*.

It can be seen therefore that as long as the percentage changes are small the difference in results between the two methods is quite small.

BIBLIOGRAPHY

BLAUG, MARK (1968). *Economic Theory in Retrospect*. London, Heinemann.

CLARK, COLIN (1967). *Population Growth and Land Use*. London, Macmillan.

HIRSCHMAN, A. O. (1958). *The Strategy of Economic Development*. Yale University Press.

RUSSELL, JOHN (1954). *World Population and World Food Supplies*. London, Allen and Unwin.

UNITED NATIONS (1968). *International Action to Avert the Impending Protein Crisis*.

ACKNOWLEDGEMENTS

Grateful acknowledgement is made to the following source for material used in this unit:

United Nations for *United Nations Statistical Year Book*, 1968 Tables 167/168.

Unit 35
Population Growth and Social and Political Systems

CONTENTS UNIT 35

		PAGE
	INTRODUCTION	101
1	SOME VIEWS ABOUT POPULATION CHANGE AS A SOCIAL AND POLITICAL PROBLEM	101
2	SOME SOCIAL ASPECTS OF THE 'POPULATION PROBLEM'	105
2.1	What is the 'Problem'?	105
2.1.1	The Assumption about Unlimited Fertility in Developing Countries	106
2.1.2	The Assumption about the Birth Rate and Developing Countries	110
2.1.3	The Assumption about 'Population Pressure'	113
2.1.4	Conclusion	117
2.2	Some Detailed Problems that may Arise from the Effects of Population Increase	118
2.2.1	Pressure on Land	119
2.2.2	Pressure on Other Resources	122
2.2.3	Conclusion	123
3	POPULATION GROWTH AND ITS POLITICAL EFFECTS	124
3.1	Questioning the Conventional Wisdom	124
3.2	Political Scientists and the Breakdown of the Problem	128
3.3	Some Suggested Political Effects	131
3.4	Conclusion	133
4	GENERAL CONCLUSION	134
	ACKNOWLEDGEMENTS	135
	BIBLIOGRAPHY	136

POPULATION GROWTH AND SOCIAL AND POLITICAL SYSTEMS

INTRODUCTION

In this unit an assessment is provided by a sociologist and a political scientist of what their two disciplines can offer to an understanding of the problems arising from the 'population explosion'. The unit is divided into three main parts. The first presents a range of quotations about the nature of the population explosion, the social situation out of which it arises and its supposed social and political effects. The quotations are chosen to illustrate some of the conventional wisdom about the topic and the succeeding two parts take up aspects of this conventional wisdom. The second part deals with the social conditions surrounding population growth and assumptions about the social situation within which the problems arising from that growth have to be solved. The third goes on to consider the political effects of population growth.

In part, therefore, we are considering a substantive point about population growth and its social and political implications, but at the same time this substantive point has been taken as the basis for discussing certain points about the contribution that sociologists and political scientists can make in relation to the so-called population problem – and by extension to other social problems.

1 SOME VIEWS ABOUT POPULATION CHANGE AS A SOCIAL AND POLITICAL PROBLEM

People speak of 'a population problem' and it is appropriate to start a discussion of the social and political problems arising from population growth by elaborating what the problem is regarded as being. This is best done by quoting the words of some of those who have written or spoken about it. A starting point is provided by Sir Julian Huxley's (1956, p. 2) statement: 'the problem of population is the problem of our age'. At one period a Western audience would have interpreted this as meaning that there were difficulties arising from a declining population. Gunnar Myrdal (1940) in lectures delivered in 1938 spoke of declining population as one of the major dilemmas of the period. The British House of Commons had, the previous year, passed a resolution which began: 'This House is of the opinion that the tendency of the population to decline may well constitute a danger to the maintenance of the British Empire. . . .' (Hansard, 10 February 1937), and an important book was published in Britain at the same time, entitled *The Population Problem*, in which various experts discussed the dangers of a declining British population.[1] But now 'the population problem' has a different meaning for Western audiences – the kernel of the problem being not the fear of declining numbers amongst European nations but of rapidly increasing numbers throughout large areas of the

---

[1] T. H. Marshall (ed.) (1938), *The Population Problem: The Experts and the Public*, London, Allen and Unwin.

world. Take this editorial presented as evidence to an American Senate hearing on population:[1]

> One of the greatest problems of modern man – the population explosion and how to control it – has come out into open discussion as individual, church and state search earnestly for a solution. . . . At present rates, the world's population will double in the next 35 years. . . . Babies are being born faster than a person could name them. . . .

The starting point of today's discussion is, then, rapid population growth.

Obviously such a representation of the population problem is too simple. The problem is not just rapid population growth, but its association with other factors – notably a lack of food or other resources. Chester Bowles set out a popular opinion – though he questioned it – in evidence to the same committee:[2]

> In the past the population of most developing countries has been kept in reasonable balance by a high death rate. In India, for instance, widespread debilitating and often fatal diseases combined to curb the growth of population and to reduce the capacity of millions of people, particularly in rural areas, to produce enough food to meet their needs. In the last few years this situation has been rapidly changing. The sharp decline of cholera and smallpox, the near elimination of malaria, and steadily improving diets have combined to raise the life expectancy of the average Indian from 32 years of age in 1950 to 41 years in 1960. As a result the rate of increase in population is now 2.4 per cent annually or roughly 11m. more people each year. This situation leads many observers to assert that unless the birth rates can be reduced, India like many nations in a similar position will face mass starvation.

The problem is represented as rapid population growth and limited resources; it is the two together that present the difficulty.

There is another way of regarding the problem. More people are a problem because the existence of more people has certain social and political consequences. Manifold effects are presented as resulting from rapid population growth. Consider first a moderate statement of these in a message from President Eisenhower to Congress:[3]

> Since the earth is finite in area and physical resources, it is clear that unless something is done to bring an essential equilibrium between human requirements and available supply, there is going to be in some regions, not only a series of riotous explosions but a lowering of standards of all peoples, including our own. . . .

Here then it is suggested that population growth plus limited resources has the consequence of disorder and lowered standards. But this is only a start to the catalogue of effects attributed to population growth by public figures, journalists and academics. Take the following quotations:

> Others have pointed to the crucial nature of the problem before us – the despair of parents who have more children than they want and feel they can rear properly, and the tendency of such patterns to be self-perpetuating. . . .

---

[1] Editorial, *Enquirer and News*, Battle Creek, Michigan, 18 April 1965, U.S. Senate, Sub-Committee on Foreign Aid Expenditure of the Committee on Government Operations, 89th Congress, 1st Session, Senate Hearings, *Population Crisis*, Vol. 1, p. 28.

[2] *Ibid.*, Vol. 2 A, p. 820.

[3] *Ibid.*, Vol. 1, p. 6.

Starvation is upon the people of these countries, and political stability may well become impossible.[1]

There is not one area of political action or decision, economic social or environmental, that will not be bedevilled by the remorseless excess of human numbers as the doctors perform their miracles so that the working force has to support an increasingly disproportionate population of the unproductive young and old.[2]

Human fertility is a potent force which will control India's population destiny during the next 30 years. Should her high birth rate remain at its present level and her death rate continue to decline, India's population will more than double by 1980. . . . Sheer numbers will have thwarted that breakthrough to a better life for all envisioned by her Five Year Plans.[3]

The reason for the swift rise in population is twofold: high birth rates . . . and a decline in death rates. . . . Half the world's people suffer from hunger and malnutrition. . . . Food, not Berlin or its equivalent, could be the cause of World War III. . . .[4]

As the rise of European nationalism after the French revolution coincided with the first great population increases in modern history, so now it is Asia, Africa and South America that are experiencing the population explosion, and it is in these continents that we are witnessing the upsurge of chauvinistic and imperialistic nationalism.[5]

How did a calm and peaceful little part of Asia [Kerala in Southern India] come to be such a hotbed of communism? There are a number of complicated answers to this question, based on history, politics and economics. But two underlying reasons stand out. The first is a physical fact: Kerala is so overcrowded that its people simply do not have enough food to keep their living above the concentration camp level.[6]

As population continues to increase more rapidly than ability to satisfy needs and desires, political unrest perhaps leading to the overthrow of existing governments, becomes almost inevitable.[7]

Many of the political problems we are suffering throughout the world can be laid at the doorstep of the population explosion and its attendant miseries. We cannot convince nations of the wisdom of our democratic way of life if they are suffering from growth problems that no system can cure, and, in the process of attempting to adopt our methods, even with our help, they continue to drop further into the clutches of hunger and misery.[8]

---

1 *Ibid.*, evidence of Representative Paul H. Todd, Vol. 1, p. 26.

2 David Wood in *The Times*, 8 March 1971, p. 13.

3 'India: High Cost of Fertility', Population Reference Bureau, *Population Bulletin*, December 1958.

4 Editorial, *Enquirer and News*, Battle Creek, Michigan, 18 April 1965, *loc. cit.*

5 H. S. Commager, 'Overpopulation and the new nations', in Fairfield Osborn (ed.), *Our Crowded Planet: Essays on the Pressures of Population*, New York, Doubleday, 1962, p. 119.

6 John Robbins, *Too Many Asians*, New York, Doubleday, 1959, p. 12.

7 H. F. Dorn, 'World population growth', in P. M. Hauser (ed.), *The Population Dilemma*, Englewood Cliffs, New Jersey, Prentice-Hall Inc.

8 U.S. Senate, Sub-Committee on Foreign Aid expenditure, *op. cit.*, Vol. 1, p. 130. Evidence of Representative George E. Brown.

> .... the pervasive and depressive effect that uncontrolled growth of population can have on many aspects of human welfare. Nearly all our economic, social and political problems become more difficult to solve in the face of uncontrolled population growth.[1]

A whole range of social, economic and political ills are presented in these quotations as being unalterably connected with population growth. The population problem, it would appear, has tentacles spreading right through society.

Summing up so far then, we see that the term 'population problem' is merely a piece of conversational shorthand. On occasions it describes the phenomenon of rapid population growth, on others a variety of supposed economic, social and political consequences of that growth. At yet other times it refers to the problem of controlling that growth. With respect to this issue, the recurring theme is of something that is a biological process.

> Human fertility is a potent force.[2]

> It is widely recognised that the growth and control of human populations is the major biological problem overshadowing the second half of the twentieth century.[3]

> The population problem is the result of our new knowledge of public health. . . . The medical knowledge which has so increased the lifespan came before the two most important developments which now give us the knowledge and means to plan families. These developments are the pill and the coil.[4]

> In our judgement, this problem can be successfully attacked by developing new methods of fertility regulation and implementing programs of voluntary family planning widely and rapidly throughout the world.[5]

> Quite obviously any comprehensive program for solving population problems . . . must seek to enhance motivation and also to improve procedures for voluntary control of fertility. A broadly based effort to develop clearer understanding of the physiology and biochemistry of the reproductive process is a primary requirement. . . . There is a parallel need – no less important – for extensive systematic application of new basic knowledge in the development of new techniques, procedures, devices, and medically active compounds for the regulation of fertility.[6]

This is simply one statement of the common argument that procreation is a biological and physiological process and as such, checking growth is fundamentally a biological and physiological problem. As the last sentence of the above quotation indicates, the contribution of social science is according to this view to help to spread acceptance of new practices designed to deal with the true nature of the problem.

---

1 Committee on Science and Public Policy of the National Academy of Sciences (1963), *The Growth of World Population*, National Research Council, p. 175.

2 'India: High Cost of Fertility', *op. cit.* (1970).

3 Book description on cover of A. Allison (ed.) (1970), *Population Control*, Harmondsworth, Penguin Books Ltd.

4 Sub-Committee Hearings, *op. cit.*, evidence of Representative Paul H. Todd, p. 26.

5 Committee on Science and Public Policy of the National Academy of Sciences, *The Growth of World Population*, National Research Council, 1963, p. 139.

6 *Ibid.*, p. 175.

To sum up then, there are many authoritative sounding pronouncements about the population problem facing the world. In the 1960s and early 1970s, in contrast to thirty years ago, what is common to these is concern at the rate of population growth. This is part of what is presented as being a problem – to some it is the problem itself, but more generally there are two other components to the problem. First, the effects which are far-reaching, and second, the difficulty of achieving a slowing-up in the pace at which people multiply.

Aspects of the 'problem' fall within the province of particular disciplines. The 'breaking down' of social phenomena, so as to facilitate analysis, is, of course, one of the factors underlying the development of the individual disciplines, a point you may remember from the first radio programme associated with this course. Thus some economic aspects have been dealt with in Unit 34, whilst the remainder of this unit will consider some social and political ones. The element of social engineering inherent in the birth control aspect will be dealt with by a social psychologist in Unit 36.

"Guess what, mother? We're expecting another bundle of joy!"

Figure 35.1

2 SOME SOCIAL ASPECTS OF THE 'POPULATION PROBLEM'

2.1 What is the 'Problem'?

The first step to take in discussing any problem, as we have already indicated, is to find out what the 'problem' really consists of – for it may not be so simple as would appear from the many confident assertions given above on pp. 102–4. Only after having clarified the problem (and discovered, incidentally, something of its complexity), is it possible to go on to discuss in detail some of the specific problems involved in what is usually called for short – 'the population explosion'.

In this section therefore we shall be looking at the assumptions behind some of the pronouncements, cited above, on the subject of the population explosion and suggesting that some of these at least give a rather misleading impression of the actual facts. You will find that two themes running through the discussion are first, the significance of humanly-controlled *social* factors (as distinct from immutable physical causes); and second, the difficulty of disentangling single causes from the complex interrelated web of reality – both themes that fit well into the general tenor of the sociology units throughout the course.

One common view of the population problem appears to be as follows. In most developing nations the birth rate is far too high with the result that there is population pressure – in other words, just too many people. This inevitably has vast social, political and economic effects, most, or all of them, for the worse – 'the population problem and its attendant miseries' as it was put by the United States politician cited above (p. 103). The area that seems to spring most readily to mind here is South Asia, particularly India. The solution seems obvious. What is needed is for Western nations to propagate birth control methods in such countries in order to limit the birth rate. Without this people in India and other underdeveloped areas will continue, from both ignorance and unwillingness to change, to breed to the limit, and the resultant population pressure will inevitably bring disaster.

"These birds and bees – why don't they use the Pill?"

Figure 35.2

This analysis (and the associated solution) of the 'population problem' is not, of course, held by everyone. But it is common enough to be classed as a popular view of the matter, and in one form or another, is continually cropping up in much writing and propaganda on the subject as the quotations on pp. 102–4 indicated.

A social scientist is a bit more suspicious however.[1] He knows that he can never take for granted that the popular definition of a problem is necessarily correct.[2] So the first thing he does is to look at the various assumptions in the popular view, to see if they are justified and, as part of this, to try to get the problem in perspective. For obviously until we know just what the 'problem' is it is fruitless to rush in to talk about a possible 'solution'.

2.1.1 THE ASSUMPTION ABOUT UNLIMITED FERTILITY IN DEVELOPING COUNTRIES

Part of the popular view is that people are somehow 'breeding to the limit' in many developing countries. There is 'uncontrolled population growth' and the problem is a 'biological' one.[3] The picture is of

---

[1] One good description of sociology is 'the art of mistrust' (P. L. Berger, *Invitation to Sociology*, Harmondsworth, Penguin Books Ltd., 1966, p. 42). This is a very relevant side of both sociology and political science for the discussion here.

[2] A point that has come into a number of earlier units, e.g. the way the sociologist has to point out that popular assumptions about 'the decline of the family' in Britain rest on mistaken assumptions (Unit 9).

[3] See quotations on p. 104 above.

people subject merely to uncontrolled biological forces, living somehow on the threshold of nature. Such people, according to this model, must be instructed in the idea of birth control and taught how to use appropriate devices. Otherwise they will continue to breed unchecked.

Now this view is in fact false. *All* populations already have their own norms for regulating both fertility and the size of the resulting population. It used to be assumed that 'primitive' populations bred to near the biologically possible maximum. Recent study, however, of the demography of such communities has shown that this belief is unfounded: 'the influence of social and perhaps even psychological factors becomes dominant. In all the communities studied the average number of children born to women over the reproductive period is much lower than the maximum possible'.[1] This is discussed in more detail in the prescribed reading by Chinoy[2] and by Freedman,[3] but briefly the point is that fertility is always to some extent a *socially* controlled process, both because of social norms regulating fertility in general, and because having children is in all societies a motivated act.

"We've really enjoyed this little get—together, Effie. You must have another baby soon!"

Figure 35.3   A socially motivated act.

In various areas of the world, for instance, social controls were and are applied to population growth[4] by such socially approved customs as lengthy suckling, spacing children through deliberate abstinence (specially in polygynous societies), infanticide in certain circumstances, whether overt or disguised, or abortion. Other social norms may encourage a high birth rate, like, for instance, the prestige or economic value[5] of a large family. Many other social factors too are almost certainly correlated with the birth rate, even though the exact relationship may be unclear – like religious beliefs, for instance, age of marriage, social class, economic background, amount of education,

---

1   W. Brass, 'The growth of world population' in A. Allison (ed.), *Population Control*, Harmondsworth, Penguin Books Ltd, 1970, p. 134.

2   Chinoy (1970), chapter 17, especially pp. 433–40.

3   R. Freedman, 'Norms for family size in underdeveloped areas', *Proceedings of the Royal Society*, Series B, 159, 1963. (Reprinted in *Reader*, pp. 655 ff.)

4   See Unit 36, p. 167.

5   See Unit 34, pp. 177–8.

With changes in these factors, furthermore, it seems that demographic patterns are also liable to change. Even when the exact relationships are unclear, it is certain that fertility is in all countries very much a socially controlled process.

Population in India can be taken as one example here (further examples are explored in the readings just mentioned). If we are to understand the process of fertility in India, we have to consider a large number of *non*-biological factors. We cannot just point to 'human fertility (as) a potent force'[1] or the need for 'clearer understanding of the physiology and biochemistry of the reproductive process'.[2] One must also consider social factors like, for example, the near-universality of marriage, which is a quasi-religious duty, and the generally early age of marriage. There is also the social ban on the re-marriage of widows (these women are 'socially sterilised' as one commentator puts it[3]), and the value placed on the tradition of the Hindu joint family. Again, there is the emphasis placed on having sons, partly for religious reasons, partly for economic, for in many peasant-farming situations the labour provided by family members represents one of the main forms of wealth.[4] There are also locally held ideas about the ideal size of families probably at least partly related to the known high rate of death among young children, so that to achieve even a moderately sized family it is not unreasonable to adopt the insurance policy of a large number of births.[5]

Now these social factors – among others – cut several ways, even though the main emphasis is, in practice, on the factors encouraging fairly high fertility. Some, like the ban on widow re-marriage, may reduce over-all fertility, while the preference for sons rather than daughters (and therefore probably greater care – and thus lower mortality – of male than female children) may help to explain the higher number of men than women in the population over-all.

"A boy at last! It'll be a great help when he gets a paper round"

Figure 35.4 *The desire for sons.*

---

1 As it is put in an earlier quotation, p. 104.

2 See earlier quotation on p. 104.

3 S. Chandrasekhar, *Population and Planned Parenthood in India*, London, Allen and Unwin, 2nd ed. 1961, p. 39. This situation is now gradually changing.

4 One example of this is illustrated from the village of Andheri in northern India shown on television programme 35. See also the discussion of the law of diminishing returns in Unit 34, p. 81, and the analysis of children as an investment good in Unit 32, p. 27.

5 For 'ideal' sizes of family in India see Unit 36, p. 159, and the *Reader*, p. 665.

Other factors, like the religious and economic ones, probably encourage fertility. Others again arouse particular argument, like the controversy over whether early marriage does or does not encourage greater fertility.[1] In fact, the exact effect of all these social factors on fertility is controversial and uncertain – so too is the extent to which their effect is or is not consciously recognised by the people concerned. What is certain, however, is that they do have some effect and that the process of having children is not determined by purely biological forces.[2]

A further point should be added here. This is that the over-all population size (and hence rate of increase or decrease) is not merely a function of fertility (and mortality) rates, but also of population movement.[3] Migration, whether internal or external, can affect the 'population pressure' in any given country, and this too is a process that is clearly a socially rather than a biologically controlled one.

So it is far too simple and misleading a picture merely to think of people in underdeveloped (or any) nations somehow breeding unchecked, subject to biological not social forces, with the implication that social norms on the matter must be introduced from the outside, i.e. from Western nations. The 'problem' is defined as preventing this unchecked breeding, and the solution seen as the introduction of control of births through certain contraceptive techniques, drawn from the West.[4] This then, in turn, is seen as leading to another problem – how to get across these new techniques; the 'problem of innovation' considered in the next unit.

But, as already argued, such an assumption mis-states the 'problem'. People in all populations already have their own means of controlling births (whether at a relatively high or a relatively low level, depending on the society), through norms about the ideal family size or through various other social factors (perhaps not consciously recognised) that affect fertility. The 'problem' of changing fertility patterns is not, then, only or primarily a biological one[5] – a matter of the innovation of new mechanical techniques. It is, more significantly, a matter of the accepted norms, and other social factors which, in a number of developing countries (at least at certain points in history), encourage high fertility. Without a change in these, techniques of whatever kind can have little effect. Obviously, then, if the 'problem' is seen as high fertility, the solution has to be seen in terms of changing the social norms and social con-

---

1 On this controversy, see Hawthorn (1970), p. 27, and the mention in television programme 32. The assertion that it did is, of course, the crux of Malthus' argument. See Unit 34, p. 77.

2 This reminds us again of man as a social (not purely biological) animal (see Unit 5).

3 For a further discussion of this, see Unit 33, pp. 41–2, and W. Zelinsky (1966), *A Prologue to Population Geography*, Englewood Cliffs, New Jersey, Prentice-Hall Inc., especially pp. 43 ff.

4 One solution that is sometimes proposed is a birth control pill (an increasingly popular technique in the West in the 1960s) cheap enough to be used widely in the developing countries. So far this has proved impracticable and the IUD has been favoured – for economic reasons (it is extremely cheap) and for psychological ones (once *in situ* it is usually effective for a long period and, therefore, unlike the pill or the condom does not require continuous motivation).

5 As assumed in the earlier quotations about population growth and control being a 'major biological problem'.

ditions which make for high fertility. In such a change, particular techniques of birth control, from wherever they are imported, are only one factor. To concentrate exclusively on this is to fall into what has been well termed 'the technological fallacy which has long marked Western thinking in this area . . . in other words, a kind of blind faith in the gadgetry of contraception.'[1] What the sociologist can contribute in this situation is to try to isolate other social factors as well which affect fertility so that, if government or other agencies wish to influence the birth rate, they can pay attention to these as well as (or in addition to) the currently fashionable mechanical techniques.

The sorts of social factors that may be involved are discussed further in the reading,[2] but they are of course likely to vary in detail according to the detailed conditions in each area. The sociologist thus often finds himself in the position of insisting that there are no short-cut and easy answers without taking account of the particular social conditions of each case.

Figure 35.5   The operation of social pressures.

2.1.2   THE ASSUMPTION ABOUT THE BIRTH RATE AND DEVELOPING COUNTRIES

A second assumption in the popular view is that the main focus of interest when considering the 'population problem' needs to be on the high birth rate of the 'developing' nations (like, for example, India, Africa or China). This assumption needs to be looked at carefully, for though there are certainly elements of truth in it, it is also in some ways misleading.

Some statistical measures of fertility and mortality have been discussed in Unit 32, whilst recent figures for many countries appear in Zelinsky (1966, pp. 139–41) and the *Reader* (pp. 617–19). Put briefly, the facts are that the world's population has been increasing rapidly in recent years but that the increase has not been uniform for all countries. By and large it has been most rapid in the so-called 'developing' countries with high birth rates, but this is not true of

---

1   L. F. Schnore, 'Social problems in the underdeveloped areas: an ecological view', *Social Problems*, 8, 1961, p. 187.

2   Also, for further discussion, see the classic article by K. Davis and J. Blake, 'Social structures and fertility: an analytic framework', *Economic Development and Social Change*, 4, 3, 1956 (summarised in *Reader*, p. 667); also W. Zelinsky, *op. cit.*, Chapter 6, and B. Benedict, 'Population regulation in primitive societies', in A. Allison (ed.), *Population Control*, Penguin, 1970. See also Unit 36, p. 167.

all such countries, nor have all the 'developed' countries either static or slowly growing populations.

Broadly speaking, it is true that population growth is at its most rapid amongst the economically underdeveloped countries.[1] However, one must look with care at this, for the situation is more complex than just attributing everything to the high birth rates of developing countries would suggest.

First it is not a high birth rate alone, but the combination of this with a falling death rate, that is involved. With the spread of medical science and public health measures, like the use of D.D.T., more people have survived and survived longer. This in combination with a continuing high birth rate has an obvious result: rapid population growth.

Second, the size of the base population is relevant. Where this is large already (as, say, in India or China), the annual population increment is also very large. In India, for instance, it amounts to some thirteen millions. It is this juxtaposition of an already large population that is densely settled (in terms of both land and other resources) *and* a rapid rate of population growth (say two and a half per cent per annum), that rivets world attention on a country such as India. Other areas with even more rapid rates of population growth – Latin America for instance – sometimes have lower base populations and lower densities. There the absolute increases tend to be less startling. The crucial factor here, then, is absolute population size rather than relative birth rates.

A third factor also needs to be noted, the question of 'population pressure'. If one looks at the over-all (as distinct from regional) figures, it is as high in parts of Western Europe as in, say, India or China.[2] But there is a big difference: the amount of resources. In much of Western Europe, the base population and densities may be high – but these countries tend to have greater resources and the means of exploiting them, in contrast to the relative poverty of many developing countries.

Some of the assumptions mentioned in this section can be seen in greater perspective if we look at some of the changing popular attitudes to the 'population problem' in India. In so far as one can date the population explosion in India, it appears to have begun in the 1930s (Table 1). And yet it has been the fashion ever since Malthus to talk of the great population increase in India and consequent misery of the Indian people.[3] In 1800 for example the Abbé Dubois wrote of India:

> Of these causes [of the misery of the lower classes] the chief one is the rapid increase in population . . . a considerable increase in the population should be looked upon as a calamity rather than a blessing.[4]

Similarly, a book published in 1929 argues that population increase is the chief obstacle to economic progress in India. 'The population

---

1 For statistical illustrations of the points being made in this part of the unit see Zelinsky (1966), pp. 139–42.

2 According to *United Nations Demographic Yearbook 1969*, p. 83, over-all density figures (population per square kilometre) were South Asia 67, Europe 92.

3 For this and much of the following discussion see Davis (1968), p. 203.

4 *Hindu Manners, Customs and Ceremonies*. trans. and ed. H. K. Beauchamp, 3rd ed. Clarendon Press, Oxford, 1924, pp. 93–4.

TABLE 1

The growth of population in India 1901-1971

Census Year	Total Population (in millions)	Rate of increase between censuses
1901	238	
1911	252	5·9%
1921	251	−0·4%
1931	279	7·2%
1941	319	14·4%
1951	361	13·2%
1961	439	21·6%
1971	547	24·6%

1 The figures for 1901–1961 from A. Chandra Sekhar (1971), 'Some aspects of the urbanisation of population in India', *Proceedings of the International Population Conference 1969*, Vol. iv, p. 2883. Liege. The International Union for the Scientific Study of Population.

problem lies at the root of the whole question of India's economic future.'[1] Similar explanations of India's poverty in terms of over-population were common throughout the nineteenth and early twentieth centuries,[2] and the quotations relating to India on p. 103 are only recent examples of a long continuing attitude. This fashion in interpreting the situation naturally received extra support from the common attitude, both in the nineteenth century and later, that the poverty of the poor was basically to be attributed to their own improvidence. This attitude seems to come particularly easily to those who feel themselves in some way responsible for the people living in such poverty – as the British were for many years for the peoples of India.

One group that was particularly suspicious of this attitude were the Indian nationalist leaders of the 1940s – and here we come to the second fashion in interpretation. They took the line that all this propaganda about the 'population problem' in India was a mere red herring introduced to hinder plans for independence. They regarded such interpretation as a 'myth', a 'fallacy', a 'fable' (Davis, 1968, p. 204). They were reacting, perhaps, to the evaluative overtones of the first attitude; and this was (and is) understandable enough. But in doing so they in turn tended to gloss over the more recent figures which did genuinely show a rapid population increase for India as a whole: so that this attitude too had its emotive side. While the present policy of the Indian government with its emphasis on 'stabilising the growth of population'[3] does not accept this interpretation, the general attitude that the basic problem is not primarily population increase but poverty or poor use of resources is one that is still held in many circles.[4]

Clearly then the nature of the 'population problem' is by no means

---

1 V. Anstey, *The Economic Development of India*, London, Longmans, 1929, p. 474.

2 See Davis, *op. cit.*, pp. 203–4.

3 India Planning Commission, *Third Five Year Plan*, New Delhi, 1961, p. 675.

4 Marxists, for instance, often deny the possibility of a 'population problem' in terms of over-population. See also the discussion of the economic aspects of the 'problem' and the resulting controversies in Unit 34.

self-evident but involves a careful interpretation and analysis of the evidence (much of which is itself in dispute)[1]. In particular, the assumption that the 'problem' is basically a matter of developing nations and their specially high birth rate turns out to be an over-simplified one. Even if one does choose to focus mainly on developing nations (and there are reasons given later why even this is hardly a balanced approach), there are many other factors at work besides the birth rate: the increase because of falling mortality rates, the large absolute numbers often involved and the relative poverty and lack of material resources in many other countries. When one also has to sort out the political or evaluative overtones built into many interpretations, it becomes clear that the whole 'problem' is an extremely complex one, an aspect to which the simple assumption we started with does little justice.

2.1.3 THE ASSUMPTION ABOUT 'POPULATION PRESSURE'

Another strand in the popular view of the 'population problem' concerns the existence of 'population pressure'. Put crudely, the assumption is that in certain areas of the world (and these are usually assumed to coincide with the 'developing' world) there are just far too many people and this fact inevitably causes 'problems': the 'remorseless excess of human numbers' and the inevitability of 'mass starvation' (see above, pp. 102–3).

"One–third of the world starving, and YOU'RE feeding your SKIN!"

Figure 35.6 The effect of population pressure.

This assumption too needs to be looked at rather carefully. Again there are clearly some elements of truth in it, but at the same time, stated in this way it draws a very over-simplified picture of reality.

In the first place large and increasing numbers of people do not self-evidently present a 'problem'. From the point of view of governmental population policies, the opposite – a too small or declining population – has far more often been regarded as 'the problem'. In fact, there is a long history of government legislation designed to affect fertility; till recent times almost all of it has been pro-natalist, i.e. intended to increase fertility. From the Babylonian Code of Hammurabi in the twentieth century B.C. to the drive to raise the birth rate in Nazi Germany or the post-war USSR, or the

---

1 For further discussion of the difficulty of collecting and analysing precise figures in this area, see Unit 32.

system of family allowances in many modern countries, governments have often made it part of their policy to encourage population increase (or, at least, prevent its decrease).[1] More recently, some governments have started to introduce explicitly anti-natalist policies, among them post-war Japan, whose standard of living had fallen drastically during the war, and the Indian government since 1952 (particularly since 1961). On the other hand, France still has a strongly pro-natalist policy, Sweden a moderately pro-natalist one, while in China there have been fluctuating policies about whether or not to discourage fertility.

Governments, in other words, have not necessarily found population size a clear-cut or a constant 'problem'. Some have taken one line, some another, others have had different policies at different times. The point here is that they have seen their interests in different directions, partly because of the differing political principles and the real controversies involved about the advantages or otherwise of a rising population (discussed in Unit 34), partly because of their differing situations and resources. From this point of view, then, 'population pressure' cannot necessarily be assumed to be a self-evident 'problem' but only to be one in so far as it is seen as such by particular groups in relation to their own objectives and resources.

This leads on to a second main point. This is that the idea of 'population pressure', of too many people, is necessarily a relative idea; the pressure must be *on* something. Put another way, one could ask: too many people for what? 'Population pressure' is not an absolute, but must be seen as a kind of balance between population size on the one hand and the resources available to it on the other.

Now it is obvious that resources vary both between and within countries. The sort of density, for instance, that would strain even basic food resources to the utmost in a peasant area dependent primarily on farmland, might be quite acceptable as far as food goes in a wealthy and technologically developed city.[2] Again the resources available to 'developed' (i.e. wealthy) nations in many respects greatly exceed those available in poorer nations with an immediate effect on the equation between population/resources, and so on whether or not there is 'population pressure'. The balance in terms of land and other natural resources is by no means the same in all 'underdeveloped countries'. In some, like Latin America or much of Africa, the present population is specially sparse, so despite the rapid increase (Latin America's is probably the highest in the world), there is no over-all prospect of 'population pressure' for some time.[3] In fact, some economists would even argue that one of the resources such countries sometimes lack in order to exploit their environment fully is, precisely, more population.[4] The variations within a single country too can be striking. Geddes and Learmonth, for instance, have indicated the differences in the balance between population and resources in different parts of India.[5] This is also illustrated in

---

[1] For some further details and references see Heer (1968), pp. 102 ff.

[2] For some further elaboration of this see Myint in *Reader*, p. 646.

[3] Though in both cases there are localised pockets of very high population density.

[4] Myint, *loc. cit.*

[5] *Reader*, pp. 620 ff.

the television programme accompanying this unit, where the crowded conditions of Calcutta form a contrast with the northern Indian village of Andheri where there is still plenty of land to go around and the scarce resource is people to work it.[1]

One cannot, therefore, generalise about 'population pressure', whether in developing or in developed countries. This becomes even more obvious when one remembers that 'resources' are not something given once and for all but comprise *known* and *exploited* resources. This exploitation may well vary as between different populations, and certainly varies at different periods of history. Thus technological advance – in other words an increasing control and exploitation of certain resources – has made it possible for certain areas (and, indeed, the world as a whole) to support a far higher density of population than would otherwise have been possible, by altering the equation that represents 'population pressure'. In India, for instance, the so-called 'green revolution' (the development of new strains of cereal crops) of recent years has resulted in vastly increased production. It seems, in fact, that food production in the densely populated parts of Asia has (unlike Latin America) kept pace with or exceeded population growth (apart from the two years of Indian harvest failure). The 'resources' side of the equation, therefore, is not immutable, but is related to human ingenuity and

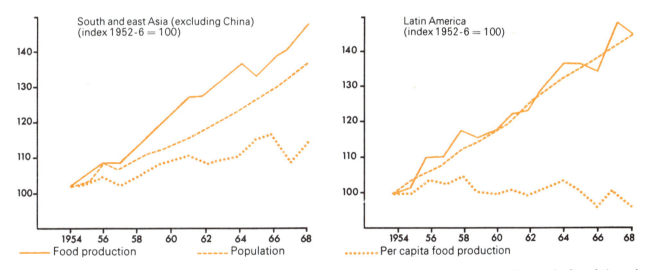

Figure 35.7 *The growth of population and of food production in Latin America and South and East Asia.*[2]

exploitation. In other words, resources are partly social and not merely geographical or biological facts.

This point comes out even more strongly when one remembers that the use of resources is not just a matter of *needs*. It is also a matter of *wants*.[3] There are many cases where resources are available in the physical sense but for various social reasons people do not choose to exploit them: they are not socially available. At a simple level for instance it is a truism that many Englishmen would rather go hungry than eat horsemeat. In many African societies, women and children

---

1 Or, alternatively, machines to allow the limited number of people to farm larger acreages.

2 Boserup, E., 'Population growth and food supplies', in Allison, A. (ed.) (1970), *Population Control*, Harmondsworth, Penguin Books Ltd., p. 162.

3 A concept discussed, among other places, in some earlier psychology and economics units.

do not care to eat eggs (a cheap and widely available source of protein) even though they are often precisely the groups most in need of protein. Similarly, in many disaster episodes, with people starving, local governments have sometimes incurred great misunderstanding from foreign aid organisations for insisting on money rather than the proffered foreign foodstuffs, on the grounds that their people – even when starving – only wanted their accustomed food. This emphasis on wants, then, applies even to something as basic as food for people near starvation level. It is also true of the many more complex ways in which we exploit socially recognised resources – which, in turn, affect the basic equation which makes up the extent of 'population pressure'.

The question of wants also means that the use of resources may go far beyond what someone from another social background might consider quite adequate for survival or even for a 'good life'. It has been calculated, for instance, that a child born in the United States is likely to consume in the course of a lifetime twenty-eight times as much as a child in India (Table 2) (Wrigley, 1969, p. 209). The Ameri-

TABLE 2

Estimated consumption per head in 1960 in various countries (United Kingdom = 100)

United States	140	Mexico	22	Ghana	8
Sweden	125	Mauritius	16	Korean Republic	6
United Kingdom	100	Taiwan	12	India	5
West Germany	86	Ceylon	9	Pakistan	4
Algeria	22				

can child will grow up in a context where certain wants in terms of consumption of electricity, gas, water or food, of car or home ownership, of various public services, and of the consequent pollution of air and land will all be socially taken for granted. The Indian child will grow up in a context where fewer wants will be recognised. Those concerned with global environmental considerations can therefore state forcibly that 'the birth of an American baby is a greater disaster for the world than that of twenty-five Indian babies.'[1] From the point of view of an analysis of 'population pressure', it can be seen that the resources side of the equation thus depends very much on people's wants and expectations. Rising expectations (and therefore increasing wants) in both developed *and* developing countries make for more pressure on resources (i.e. socially exploited resources) and thus yet again alter the equation that makes up 'population pressure'. Looked at this way, some have argued that the increasing wants and expectations of wealthy countries make them just as susceptible to 'population pressure' as poorer countries, precisely because of this greater exploitation of resources (Wrigley, 1969, p. 234).

'Population pressure', therefore, is not an absolute or a self-evident 'problem'. It is related to a number of social factors, among them governmental policies and ideologies, socially exploited re-

---

[1] Paul Ehrlich, 'Eco-catastrophe!', *Ramparts*, September 1969, p. 4.

sources, and socially recognised wants and expectations. The assumption, therefore, that 'population pressure' is something absolute and inevitable and a problem confined to the developing countries, is misleading indeed. Certainly many (not all) developing

"I'd better take two — we've just had twins!"

Figure 35.8 Population pressure on resources.

countries are poor and have large populations. But 'population pressure' is not an inevitable and immutable fact of life anywhere, is certainly not confined to developing countries, and is in many respects a socially controlled rather than a purely physical phenomenon.

2.1.4   CONCLUSION

The main conclusion of this discussion is twofold. First, the 'problem' of the 'population explosion' (and hence the 'solution') turns out to be far more complex than the simplified statement of it in the popular view set out at the beginning. In fact, in so far as it can be identified as a 'problem' at all, it is not really *one* problem but a whole series of different problems. There are problems for instance arising from poverty, problems arising from wealth, from rising wants and expectations, from large populations, from small populations, from various social prejudices about the use of particular resources, from social and governmental controls of migration, from socially sanctioned attitudes to family size – and so on.

It may seem a somewhat depressing conclusion that a sociologist has to start with stressing the complexity of the problem and the fallacy of many accepted assumptions rather than presenting a clear-cut panacea for the 'population problem'. But since, fortunately or unfortunately, the social world is a complex not a simple thing, the sociologist whose role it is to study that world is bound constantly to be pointing out its complexity, even when this makes him unpopular with those who wish for quick solutions to simple-sounding problems. In the case of the 'population problem' what he can do is to point to the *various* problems involved and make clear that what kind of solution has to be chosen by those making decisions depends on *which* of these problems they wish to tackle – some of them, perhaps, totally imaginary ones.

The second side of the conclusion is perhaps more encouraging. This is to stress the *social* rather than purely biological or physical nature of many of the problems involved. In other words, the parameters are often not inevitably fixed factors or immutable biological forces, but *social* factors[1] – and *social* factors offer far more prospect of change through *human* effort. If, for example, the problem is 'population pressure' in the sense of some imbalance between 'population' and 'resources' then there is the possibility of affecting either side of the equation: the social factors of various kinds that affect population size (in its various senses); and the social mechanisms and attitudes involved in exploiting or transferring resources.

"We're playing Mothers and Fathers – care to audition for the lodger part?"

Figure 35.9 The social nature of the problem.

Because of the social dimensions of many of the 'problems' involved, it is clear that possible solutions become much more practical than if, as is sometimes assumed, the 'population problem' was some absolute and given fact of nature. The various problems may well be difficult to solve and their solutions may well involve difficult political choices[2] – but being largely defined in terms of social factors, they are in principle susceptible to human choice and human action.

2.2 Some Detailed Problems that may Arise from the Effects of Population Increase

The general range of problems that may be involved (plus some fallacies about these) have been discussed in the first part. In this part, I am going to consider some of the more specific effects of rising population (some of which present, or are seen to present, various problems). These are effects which are likely to make themselves felt over the next generation even if the birth rate declines drastically at once; for all the people growing up in the present generation are already born. To fit the general theme of this part of the course

---

[1] You will probably have noticed the emphasis throughout this Unit on *social factors* and that this is an aspect stressed not only here but in all the sociology units in the course.

[2] This is stated, very starkly indeed, by Kingsley Davis (1967). He argues that most current family planning programmes are sociologically naive because they ignore (but see Unit 36 on this) the 'power and complexity of social life'. Further he asserts (pp. 85-6):

> if it were admitted that the creation and care of new human beings is socially motivated, like other forms of behaviour, by being a part of the system of rewards and punishments that is built into human relationships and thus is bound up with the individual's economic and personal interests, it would be apparent that the social structure and economy must be changed before a deliberate reduction in the birth rate can be achieved. . . . Since family planning is by definition private planning, it eschews any societal control over motivation. . . .

most of the examples will be drawn from India. But this does not mean that similar kinds of effects and problems do not arise elsewhere.

The first point to notice about the effect of population increase is something that will keep cropping up in the following discussion. This is the difficulty, particularly in a period of rapid social, economic and political change, of sorting out exactly which are the effects of population increase, and which of other factors.[1] Population increase, in fact, is part of a whole process of social change which in any case tends to involve, for example, more physical mobility, increasing urbanisation, new technological and educational developments, a changing political and economic scene and so on. It is very difficult to disentangle population growth and its effects from this process as a whole. This indeed may be why relatively little work has been published on the specific effects of population increase or even of population density in general. (See Heer, 1968, pp. 31ff.)

However, despite these difficulties, there are some areas in which it is reasonable to look for the effects of rising population and hence for possible 'problems' that have to be dealt with.

2.2.1 PRESSURE ON LAND

One is the problem of shortage of land. As it is put in one account (M. Smith in Srinivas, 1960, p. 176) of the situation in the Punjab (Northern India): 'With natural limits placed upon the amount of arable land available to each village, and with constantly rising population figures, the strain upon family budgets has been considerable even for land-owning joint families.' The same problem is described for Mysore (A. R. Beals in Srinivas, 1960, p. 153) at the other end of the subcontinent: 'rapid increase in population and a consequent fragmentation of land holding'. The result in Mysore has been an increasing number of farmers in the villages who find it more and more difficult to grow sufficient food for their families. Many have been faced with the prospect of emigrating or of becoming labourers on the larger farms. This shortage of land for food and even outright landlessness for large numbers of people are constantly being mentioned as problems in many areas of India.

There are a number of effects connected in turn with this factor of land shortage. One is that the fragmentation of land means smaller plots per family – which may imply not only less food production, but also sometimes less economic use of land. In Rampur, for instance, there is so much pressure on land that there is little or none available for pasture or forest. The result of this is in turn that there is little wood, so cattle dung has to be used for fuel instead of manure, and cattle must be stall-fed not pastured (Lewis, 1958, pp. 43–4). So shortage of land leads to the problems of worse use of the land that *is* available.

Landlessness has become an important factor in much political life and here too it is often seen (or presented) as a 'problem' to be tackled. This was very relevant for instance in the Vinoba Bhave movement throughout India in the 1950s, or, more recently, in Communism in Kerala. As in many other parts of the world and at

---

[1] This difficulty of isolating causes is an important methodological point in the social sciences, and applies to far more than just population. This same point is made in a different context in Unit 36, p. 168.

many periods of history, the idea of 'rights to land' and the possibility of their loss or diminution has been an emotive political slogan.

This in turn connects with the question of population movement. Students of social change in many parts of India constantly point to the connection between increasing shortage of land and migration to the towns (or elsewhere) to find money by paid work. This parallels similar movements elsewhere as well as the phenomenon of increasing urbanisation all over the world. This in turn has a whole series of political and social effects, discussed more fully later.

One difficulty here, however, is to disentangle just how far migration is in fact a direct result of 'over-population' and a resultant shortage of land. For many parts of the world it has been argued that the appeal of the 'bright lights of the town' is as important (and possibly more so) as economic pressures pushing people off the land, and that urbanisation is a world-wide process irrespective of population trends. A number of observers have commented that this may apply less to many parts of India than, say, to most areas in Africa, because of the great social value attached to land and living on the land in India. This makes many Indian peasants unwilling to move even in the face of much poverty. But there are some clear exceptions to this, like the Punjabis discussed by Geddes (the *Reader*, p. 628) among whom it has been for some time the tradition for younger sons to go off to make a living in the army. But it is in any case extremely hard to assess exactly what factors are the most influential in encouraging migration: shortage of food at home; increasing landlessness; personal ambition; the appeal of the cities. What the 'problem' leading to migration is (if there is one) will depend on which factor is the most important. Some indeed would deny that migration in itself is a 'problem' at all, but argue that the 'problem' is more *lack* of migration, in other words, the continuing high proportion of people involved in agriculture, a typical feature of 'underdeveloped' economies (see, for example, Unit 34).

Even in the 'problem' of land shortage then, which is apparently so straightforward an effect of increasing population, it is hard indeed to disentangle exactly what is the result of population increase and what of other social factors. In practice, these all seem to be bound inextricably together, so that in the actual situation it seems impossible to isolate just one of them.

There is a second difficulty too in analysing the 'problem' of population pressure. This is the point already mentioned earlier: that 'population pressure' is a relative not an absolute notion. It relates to a balance between population and exploited resources. And in this balance actual population size is only one of the factors. One must also look at the factors on the other side of the equation – the use of resources.

It has indeed been argued by a number of observers that the 'population pressure' and land shortage that can be said to exist in certain rural areas of India is due not primarily to population increase at all, but to the detailed way in which resources are distributed. In interpreting this there are, of course, many controversies, and it is possible to take various political lines. Just to illustrate the sort of possible interpretation, here is one view by Professor A. Aiyappan (1965, pp. 65–6) trying to answer the question of why so many villagers in one part of Kerala are landless:

> Is over-population the only cause of the great poverty of some villagers?...
> To answer properly, some knowledge of the land tenure and the social system supporting it is a desideratum.... I might state here in summary, that a peasantry without fixity of tenure, with little power to get their due share in the produce of the land, and therefore with little capacity to develop resources, resulted from the concentration of wealth and power in a Brahmin-landed aristocracy sharing its power with the many petty ruling chieftains and a few Nayars.... When their needs grew, they resorted to the easy way of taxing the poor giving them less and less and taking from them more and more.

One need not agree with all the details of Aiyappan's further analysis to agree that the kind of social factors he points to must be regarded as the background of any discussion of the 'resources' related to population.

The shortage of food commonly assumed to be an inevitable consequence of population increase and hence pressure on land also needs to be looked at carefully. Here again one must remember the effect of social factors on the actual exploitation of resources. For one thing, there are people's likes and dislikes in terms of food. This is not such a trivial point as it may seem. People sometimes prefer to be malnourished rather than accept a foodstuff they despise. In Kerala, for instance, tapioca is regarded as a non-prestigeful food, and the Communist Party government was nicknamed 'macaronis' in ridicule for their attempts to popularise macaroni (a good and locally available food, made of vitaminised wheat and tapioca flour) in an area of chronic malnutrition.[1] Other foodstuffs, however (including new ones), do become socially accepted. This, in conjunction with the spread of new high-yield types of grain in some states in India, is altering the socially exploited 'resources' side of the equation, and hence the standard of living possible for a given population. It must be remembered too that the resources available are constantly liable to be changing in any case in so far as this is a period of rapid social and economic change in India generally.

"You're turning that plant into a hypochondriac!"

Figure 35.10 New farming methods can affect resources.

Government action, furthermore, can affect patterns like land tenure and this too can change the general social and economic context within which one must assess 'the problem of population pressure'.

As pointed out earlier, the 'population' side of the equation too is not immutable but is susceptible to social factors. Quite apart from

---

1 Aiyappan 1965, p. 51. See the earlier discussion of 'wants' in this context (p. 116).

any change in birth or death rates, emigration is obviously one way in which population and hence 'land pressure' can be reduced. This indeed is a course that has been taken in a number of places, both in India and elsewhere. That this particular solution is not adopted more in India (or in particular parts of India) can again be connected with various social factors, none of them necessarily inevitable or permanent: the high social value attached to the land, so that people are often most reluctant to move away whatever their conditions; the shortage of paid employment for many categories of work; and the restrictionist policies on immigration adopted by the governments of many of the countries to which Indian would-be migrants might turn.

So the whole 'problem' of the effects of pressure on land in India turns out to be far more complex than it looked at first sight, and to rest on a complicated equation between population – one socially controlled factor – and resources – another socially controlled factor. This equation, or rather, this complex interaction between a number of different factors, indicates that the 'problem' is not just a matter of increases in population. The 'problem' can also be seen as involving the socially controlled exploitation and availability of resources.

2.2.2 PRESSURE ON OTHER RESOURCES

Land is not the only resource involved, though perhaps because of its emotive overtones for Western as well as Indian observers it seems to be the most often talked about. But in fact pressure on resources generally is something that is very familiar to everyone, including inhabitants of Western countries. Everyone knows – and complains – about overcrowding on the roads, queues for hospital beds, competition for jobs and educational opportunities, and so on. It is also well known that what particular resources are available and exploited at a particular time is partly a matter of a series of socially influenced and individual choices, partly due to particular choices by governments to allocate resources to one item rather than another. Once again the population/resources equation is a *socially* determined not an immutable one.

Exactly the same point applies to the 'population pressure on resources problem' in developing countries, the only single difference being that these governments are (for the most part) poorer. In some (not all) the pressure on particular resources is very heavy. In India for example there is extreme competition – and much resultant heartbreak – for places at various levels of the educational system, and, perhaps even more intense, for jobs for those with high qualifications on the completion of their education. Housing shortages in cities like Calcutta are notorious, and, as the urban population grows, are likely to become even more desperate. With a population increasing all the time, the society is faced with the prospect of having constantly to expand resources even to keep level with the existing situation.[1] But difficulties like this, and the poverty of many of the countries involved, does not alter the basically *social* nature of the equation between population and resources. Policy decisions still have to be made on whether, for instance, to spend more on arms and less on hospitals, more on technical education and less on universities, more on industrial development and less on agriculture, more on refugees and less on local inhabitants, and so on.

---

[1] For a discussion of this see Unit 34.

None of these policy choices are self-evident. Nor are the various choices people make about how to exploit the resources that are available. Yet the whole idea of 'population pressure on resources' rests on the complex interaction of all these factors and to pronounce confidently that everything is due to just one of the factors (like population increase) is to misunderstand the complexity of the facts. In so far as there is a 'problem' it cannot be attributed to population increase alone for it is a function of the complex interaction of many social factors of which population increase is only one.

2.2.3 CONCLUSION

The conclusion to emerge from this discussion is the complexity of the problem. 'The population problem' turns out to involve a whole *series* of problems and also to involve a huge range of untested assumptions and disputed interpretations. And yet until one has tested out these various assumptions and sorted out the real problems from the imaginary ones, it is fruitless to rush in with suggested solutions.

The main lessons are perhaps two. First, a point which has come again and again into the sociology sections of this course: the interrelated nature of society. Population factors are interrelated with a whole range of other social factors in society, and it is difficult indeed for either the academic social scientist or the committed reformer to disentangle them. In other words, anyone concerned with the so-called 'population problem' in any capacity needs to tread warily, remembering that population is only one facet of a total situation and that there are many factors to be taken into consideration.

Second, the various 'problems' involved are not immutable and inevitable. They vary from place to place. They involve *social* factors,[1] and, as such, they are in principle susceptible to human action. It is for the social scientist to try to analyse exactly what the various problems are and to dismiss glib generalisations and naïve definitions of them. In fact it may emerge from this that there is in fact *more* opportunity for choice, more ways of human action open, than if one swallows some of the popular assumptions. It is not, after all, an inevitable fact of life that population growth will relentlessly engulf us all, with all our resources, and all that we value in life. Furthermore, the choices are far more involved than merely deciding between the pill, the sheath or IUD as the way of warding off the 'remorseless excess of human numbers'. Depending on the facts of the particular situation and its particular problems (or, just as relevant, what are seen as its problems), choices may also include such matters as, for example: what resources should be allocated to, say, armaments and what to agricultural (or other) research and development; which wants and expectations must (or should) be satisfied and which not; what degree of population movement should be allowed or encouraged and from where to where, and which groups within the population; what value should be attached to the conservation of natural resources; how can ideals about family size be changed[2] (irrespective, that is, of what particular technological devices are used in achieving the desired family size); what changes can be made in the system of land tenure to satisfy the demands of

[1] Another theme throughout the sociology sections.

[2] A point taken up in Unit 36.

landless groups; how can people's attitudes to the use of resources be changed (e.g. to get them to exploit certain nutritious, but currently socially unacceptable, types of food); how can people be persuaded to use new crops and agricultural methods; what is the right balance between population and exploited (or potential) resources in a *given* area (in specific, not absolute terms); and so on. In other words, a number of rather different problems may be involved in different situations, and it is essential first to analyse what each one is, and then look at the range of choices open to solve it in each case.

When the sociologist queries vague or unfounded generalisations and insists on stopping to analyse precisely what a problem is in each case, then he has, in fact, made no small contribution to the solution of these problems. For, having clarified and defined them, he has opened the way for individuals, groups and governments to adopt the solutions which, with full information and freed of misleading presuppositions, they choose to be the best.

TEST 1

3 POPULATION GROWTH AND ITS POLITICAL EFFECTS[1]

The quotations in the first part of this unit which could have been extended greatly indicated that some see the population problem as something of huge political significance. The decline of the British Empire, political instability, riotous explosions, the rise of chauvinistic and imperialistic nationalism, communism in Kerala, the difficulty of convincing countries to follow a democratic way of life, a Third World War, political unrest and revolution generally, have all been regarded as attributable to the 'population explosion'. Already in this unit certain ideas implicit in those quotations have been questioned, especially the assumptions about the social situation in which population change takes place. In the process the aim has also been to show what a sociologist can contribute, in terms of specifying the problem and investigating the validity of assumptions which, in terms of the conventional wisdom may look plausible, even convincing. In this section we shall examine the supposed political effects of population change starting from those statements of supposed effects given in the quotations on pp. 102–4, and at the same time continue the exploration begun in the previous part of what contribution social scientists can make in relation to the so-called population problem.

3.1 Questioning the Conventional Wisdom

You do not have to be a political scientist or, indeed, a social scientist of any description to question the sort of statements that appear on pp. 102–4. You may even feel that some of them are not worth taking seriously. But to the accusation that we are erecting Aunt Sallies, one might point out, first, that the views expressed have enjoyed a wide currency, second, they have given rise to much public concern, and, third, even the least plausible deserve inspection to expose the reasoning behind them.

Each of the quotations presents a population cause and a political

---

1 I wish to acknowledge the stimulus provided by Weiner, M. (1969), *Political Demography: an Inquiry into the Political Consequences of Population Change*, National Academy of Sciences.

effect. With all the recent statements, the cause was a rapid growth of population, the effects were various and – the first point to note – were presented in very general terms. The existence of chauvinistic

"The feeling is mutual, I can assure you!'

Figure 35.11 *The effects of population growth are various.*

nationalism, communism, riots and disorder, revolution – each of these suggested effects covers a great range of particular circumstances and obviously an initial need is to make these generalisations more specific. Is it *all* chauvinistic nationalism; is it *all* riots, or only particular riots in particular places: and what is the time period? Presumably the Nigeria-Biafra civil war could be covered and the revolution in Indonesia that replaced Sukarno, but does it apply also to the American and French revolutions? Is the argument that the revolution in Indonesia was due to rapid population growth? The first difficulty with so many of the statements about the political effects of population growth is that they are presented as generalities and they cover so many recurring political situations.

To the extent, moreover, that the generalisations are pinned down and attached to particular events they rarely fit the conclusions drawn from empirical research. Thus, if the general statements about the way population growth is the cause of riots and revolution are applied to specific instances like the Nigeria-Biafra civil war, Indonesian revolution, or the war between East and West Pakistan, rapid population growth cannot be given as a direct reason.

In fact, many of the statements quoted on pp. 102–4 are not postulating a direct cause and effect relationship between population growth and political action. They see population growth having a political result through the medium of some other intermediate consequence, such as pressure on limited food supplies, which in turn results in communism, or disorder, or revolution. There are two different arguments, therefore: arguments about immediate, direct effects of population growth, and, secondly, indirect effects through the medium of some intermediate situation.

The second sort of generalisation is the one that is particularly difficult to validate. For to seek generalisations about the relationship between such broad states as, on the one hand, a disequilibrium between human wants and available supply, and on the other, political disorder (let alone what determines the relative importance of population growth as a cause of the state of disequilibrium) is to open up an area so general and so broad that it is, for the present anyway, beyond the capacity of political scientists to deal with.

Nevertheless something can be said in a negative way about these broad generalisations. It is possible, for example, to point to sufficient instances to indicate that the sort of generalisations that have been made are not consistent with the evidence. To start with many of the statements quoted rested on the superficially obvious idea that people will turn to revolution as their food becomes scarcer and as conditions generally worsen. Yet in so far as historians and social scientists have ventured to outline in general terms the circumstances out of which revolutions grow, one consistent observation, first made by de Tocqueville in relation to the French revolution, has been that revolutionary activity tends to develop, not when conditions are deteriorating, but when economic, social and political circumstances have been improving.[1]

Or, to take a second example, consider the observation by Commager of the coincidence of population growth and chauvinistic and imperialistic nationalism. It is an interesting observation. It is true that the two phenomena went together in much of Europe during the first half of the nineteenth century, as Commager (1962) indicates, and more recently in Indonesia, Egypt and Ghana. But there are other instances where the coincidence of sharply rising population and an upsurge of nationalism does not hold. Irish nationalism, for instance, blossomed during the second half of the nineteenth century, reaching a peak with the 1916 rebellion and the Troubles at the end of the First World War. This was a period of declining population. Contemporary Hong Kong, on the other hand, has had one of the fastest growing populations in the world, and yet through the 1950s and 1960s has not been characterised by an upsurge of chauvinistic nationalism. The coincidence is not universal, and it might therefore be said that the cause-effect relationship between population growth and nationalism remains unproven.

The same sort of point can be made about a number of the other observations in the quotations. But it may be that what is implied is not that population growth causes some intermediate state, which in its turn results in disorder or some other political consequence, but rather that population growth is a condition. Population growth is not the cause, instead it provides the situation in which something else emerges as the cause. Thus the general correlation of rapid population growth through some intermediate state with disorder is presented as helping to explain the situation in Kerala in South India. Since it is false to argue from a correlation to a cause-effect relationship the quotation could simply be drawing on knowledge about rapid population being a condition for disorder. Yet even this does not, at least on the face of it, apply in other societies. Mexico and Singapore in the post-Second World War period, to take but two examples, have experienced high rates of population growth and yet have generally been regarded as politically stable, while in the same period Argentina and Chad have not been politically stable, though they have had relatively low rates of growth. In other words, even this general correlation, implying that population growth is a necessary if not sufficient condition of political instability, is not supported by the evidence.

So far this section has been built around a consideration of the

---

[1] For an appraisal and modification of this view see Krishan Kumar (ed.) (1971), *Revolution*, p. 45. London, Weidenfeld and Nicolson.

quotations on pp. 102-4, but I wish to add at this point a quotation from a paper by P. M. Hauser (1965, pp. 65-6), taken from a standard book on population problems published in the mid-1960s:

> The larger of these nations are not apt to remain hungry and frustrated without noting the relatively sparsely settled areas in their vicinity. The nations in the South-East Asian peninsular: Burma, Thailand, and the newly formed free countries of Indo-China . . . even parts of thinly settled Africa may be subject to the aggressive action of the larger and hungrier nations as feelings of population pressure mount. Moreover, Communist China, the largest nation in the world by far, faced with . . . already heavy burdens . . . may not confine her attention only to the smaller nations within her reach.[1]

Let me at this point ask two questions about this quotation. First, what demographic data would you wish to have to assess this statement? And, secondly, what assumptions are built into this quotation about the effects of population growth?[2]

On the first question, one piece of relevant demographic information would be population densities in East and South-east Asia. According to early 1960 figures, population per square kilometre in some countries in the area were:

TABLE 3

Population per square kilometre in South-east and East Asia

Country	Year	Density per square kilometre
Burma	1963	34
Cambodia	1962	31
China	1961	74
India	1961	134
Indonesia	1961	50
Japan	1963	260
Korea: North	1960	89
Korea: South	1962	266
Laos	1963	8
Malaysia	1962	31
Nepal	1964	70
Pakistan	1961	99
Phillipines	1960	90
Taiwan	1964	333
Thailand	1960	51
Vietnam: North	1960	100
Vietnam: South	1963	89

One assumption built into the quotation is that as a population grows and becomes more dense the people become more aggressive, or possibly as an alternative formulation of the assumption, that people feel population pressure, whatever the facts about actual

---

[1] Hauser, P. M. (1965), 'Demographic dimensions in world politics', in L. K. Ng, *The Population Crisis*, Bloomington, Indiana, Indiana University Press.

[2] You might care to pause at this point and attempt to answer the two questions before continuing with the text.

growth, and this makes them more aggressive. These are points on which social psychologists have no firm evidence. Also at least on the face of it the simple interpretation of events in South-east Asia is only partly consistent with the demographic data above, applying

"Well, you asked us to pass Father down the bus!"

Figure 35.12 Feeling the effects of population pressure.

more obviously to Japan and India or even the smaller countries such as North Vietnam than to China – the one country singled out.

To sum up this section, one contribution made by political scientists to understanding the population problem and its political effects is to investigate and question conventional wisdom. This involves in the first place scrutinising the statements that express that wisdom. Here I have suggested that many of the claimed effects are so broad and sweeping that they are unprovable, and this is the more so since many of them depend on an intermediate state, with this intermediate state being the direct cause and population change only serving as an ultimate cause. Secondly, I have indicated that in so far as broad statements are specified sufficiently to be attached to actual historical events, there is as much evidence against the generalisations as for them. Cause-effect relationships between population growth and political situations which seemed self evident to some of those quoted on pp. 102–4 may ultimately be shown to be valid, but at the moment they rest on conjecture. Finally, to the extent that population growth is not implied as a cause, but as a condition, the evidence for the generalisations quoted is at best inconclusive.

TEST 2

3.2 **Political Scientists and the Breakdown of the Problem**

Another contribution that political scientists can make to exploring the relationships between population change and political situations is the more constructive one of seeing whether there is a direct connection between population growth and certain recurring political conditions. Where the relationship does not involve bringing in a general intermediate state the problem is sufficiently manageable for political scientists to explore the nature of the political effects of population growth.

Yet to do this requires first of all that the general phenomenon of population growth is specified more precisely. Let us return again to the quotation from Hauser on p. 127. What is it about population in the quotation that is significant? In the first part of the quotation, the critical point was population density – densely and sparsely populated areas. What might be implied in this part of the quotation, moreover, is that population change involves differential increases: population change being more rapid and involving greater pressure on resources in the already more densely populated areas. In the last part of the quotation, on the other hand, the critical point has ceased to be population density but absolute size. It is the absolute size of China and the presence of relatively small countries around her which is implied as being the critical fact. In other words Hauser is talking about both population size and population growth.

Population growth, in fact, covers a number of different phenomena and it is important to distinguish some of its different meanings in discussions of its political effects. First, it describes an absolute growth in the size of population and it may be the sheer size rather than the rate of growth that is significant. Both will, generally speaking, result in greater population density and it may be this which has certain postulated political effects. Thus, after the Second World War, Harari African township in Salisbury, Southern Rhodesia, became the nurturing ground for increasingly radical African political movements. It coincided with rapid growth in the population of the township, and also with growing overcrowding in the available accommodation. Whether the political activities in the township were caused by the population growth was one question, and if so whether population growth in this context meant the growth in absolute numbers or greater density (if the two could be separated) was another. The political significance of population growth then may stem from an absolute growth in numbers, or alternatively, greater density.

Population growth may, alternatively, have significant effects because it brings about a change in the balance between one segment of the population and another. Population growth may involve a differential increase in one part of the population over another. For example, population growth in Northern Ireland may be more rapid among Catholics than among Protestants so affecting the balance between two communities, and it may be this rather than the absolute growth that is significant politically.

The situation in Northern Ireland is simply one example of something that is widely treated as a politically significant situation. Differential fertility between Catholics and non-Catholics in the United States – and papal opposition to birth control – gave rise to political controversy, as the proportion of Catholics steadily increased.[1] The same is true of the relative fertility of blacks and whites in the United States and of Maoris and whites in New Zealand. In the Lebanon, the government declines to record religion in the census for fear that it would show a change in the balance of Moslems and Christians and thus disturb the delicate basis on which succeeding governments have been organised. In Nigeria the figures given in the first national census after independence had to be withdrawn and a new census taken to produce more politically acceptable totals after the first had suggested a significant shift in the balance of population between the regions of the Federation. What is politically significant in each of these situations is that population growth involved a change in relative numbers between communities or groups in the population.

---

[1] 'The impact of uncontrolled birth on our democratic process', *Humanist* (January–February 1961), p. 5.

In addition to the ones already set out, population growth covers two other important demographic situations. The first is its effect on family size. Population growth means larger families, whether it is more babies in the family or more aged or both and in certain

"Tell me quick – how many?"

Figure 35.13 Large families.

circumstances, particularly where the family is an important political unit, it may be this aspect of population growth which has political or governmental consequences. Lastly, population growth involves changes in the age structure of the population. If the growth is due to an increase in the expectation of life of old people there will be more people over, say, sixty-five in the population and one consequence is that the retired or old age pensioners may become a significant factor in elections. In Britain it has become the recurring practice for both parties to seek to attach this group, and one of the more striking cases in recent years elsewhere was the appeal specifically made to them by Senator Goldwater in the 1964 presidential election campaign in the United States. In most developing countries population growth has resulted in an increase in the proportion of young people so that in many of them, more than half the population is under the age of twenty. The significance of this is discussed below.

There is, however, just one final point that needs to be made. Demographic data is nice hard data to work with. It is definite or seems so.[1] You can discover how many people there are, what is average family size, you may even be able to find out how many Hindi-speaking people there are in India (if you can agree on what Hindi covers as a language). But even where figures are not invented for political reasons – as indeed are some of the figures in the *United Nations Demographic Yearbook*[2] – even where, that is, what looks like hard data is not a politically invented, or administratively convenient, creation, it may be that the hard data is not what is significant for establishing that population change and certain political conditions are connected. What may be important is what people think.

Frequently, it is not the hard data itself that has political consequences, it is what people *think* is the data. In British politics in the

---

1 But see Unit 32 on how difficult it is to be *certain* about such figures.

2 See the comment above, p. 129, on the unacceptability of the first Nigerian census to many politicians.

1960s, for example, there was a certain amount of argument about the exact number of coloured children in the population. It is probably not too much of an exaggeration to say that some of the politicians' statements were designed primarily to make people think that the coloured population presented a threat. For what was significant for certain politicians in their campaigns for election or advancement in their party, was that people should think that coloured people were a menace and that opponents of coloured immigration or advocates of repatriation should, therefore, be

"Molly! How many kids have we now?"

Figure 35.14 Demographic data is nice hard data because you can find out how many people there are.

elected or promoted. Indeed in many political situations it is not the actual situation that is significant, but what people think to be the situation and what they think about it.

This section has been designed to show that what is meant by population change has to be specified if there is to be an understanding of its political effects. Population growth covers a number of different situations each of which may, as the illustrations have shown, have political significance, and it is important therefore to break the question down and specify whether it is growth in absolute numbers, greater density, increased family size, a change in the balance in the population, or changed age structure that provides the starting point. Equally important it is necessary to consider whether the significant cause is the fact of change, or whether it is the perception of change and attitudes towards it.

TEST 3

3.3 Some Suggested Political Effects

In the first part of this unit we indicated that a belief in the general effects of population growth was widespread. In this, the third part of the unit, it is the supposed political effects that have been considered. The argument so far has been that many of the statements that were cited on pp. 102–4 are too general, or too imprecise for their validity to be tested and established. Furthermore we have argued that if any worthwhile generalisations are to be drawn from human experience then, as a precondition for exact investigation, the problem must be broken down. It must be clear as to whether a population state is a cause or a necessary condition, and what feature of population change is being investigated must be specified.

For political scientists, the exploration of valid generalisations about the effects of some aspect of population growth or the conditions it creates is at an early stage. Since Aristotle and Plato, if not earlier, different issues connected with politics and population have been discussed. With Aristotle it was the relationship of population growth and civil disorder, with Plato the right size of population for a particular sort of government, an issue more recently considered by Rousseau and Mill. But, despite the fact that the debates can be traced back many centuries, empirical research on the political effects of population change has only been actively promoted as concern has grown about the so-called population explosion.

Necessarily with research at an exploratory stage there are as yet no broad validated generalisations to complement sceptical writing on conventional wisdom, or attempts at defining the issues to be investigated. Where empirical research has been undertaken attention is directed to specific issues. The sort of enquiry currently being conducted is illustrated by Myron Weiner's article in the *Reader*. Weiner started from an investigation of what might be described as the conventional wisdom among academic social scientists – the idea that violent political action in the urban areas of many developing countries was the result of migration and a feature of migrants, behaviour – and he investigated the validity of this assumption in one city: Calcutta. The article illustrates an assumption about the effects of population change, how the assumption can be explored, and the sort of conclusion that emerges.

The second example is of a hypothesis being set up for discussion. Herbert Moller (1968) has argued that 'irrespective of social and economic conditions, an increase in the number of youth in any society involves an increase in social turbulence'. This is a hypothesis that Moller presents on the basis of a series of examples from European and American history. There is first the point that a sharp increase in the number of young adults in what is now modern Germany came at the time of the Reformation and Peasants Revolt of 1524–5. Again, the French Revolution coincided with a period in France when forty per cent of the French population was between the ages of twenty and forty, and Moller comments (1968, p. 240) 'exposed to the economic hardships that prevailed between 1785 and 1794, the numerous under-employed young people formed an explosive population group. Their presence contributed decisively to the revolutionary unrest in city and country, and also to the military ventures of the Revolutionary and Napoleonic wars.' A marked rise in the proportion of young adults was also a characteristic of Italy when Mazzini was organising the 'Young Italy' movement, of Russia and other countries of Eastern Europe at the end of the nineteenth and early twentieth centuries, of Germany during the rise of Hitler and of the United States during the 1960s. If there is any validity in the hypothesis moreover it has considerable current significance given the situation in developing countries, for in many of these countries the proportion of young adults in the population is markedly higher than in any of the countries in Europe in which an increase in the proportion of young adults has been correlated with revolutionary situations. Thus, whereas in France in 1776 those between fifteen and twenty-nine constituted sixty-five per cent of the group thirty years and over, in Ceylon during the 1960s it was seventy per cent, Brazil and Ghana eighty per cent, Tanzania and the Philippines ninety-six per cent. Moreover, this proportion is increasing and in many developing countries there will be more young adults between fifteen and twenty-nine than there will be people thirty years and over.

Moller's hypothesis is one that Myron Weiner has discussed. Weiner has considered it as one not about the cause of revolutionary activity, but as one concerning the conditions out of which such activity arises or is likely to arise. Taking the situation in developing countries he asks[1]:

> Do these figures necessarily mean that Asia, Africa, and Latin America are destined to have a more turbulent political life than that experienced by Europe and America in the 19th century? Much depends upon the extent to which political attitudes and behavior are age-linked and the extent to which these links transcend cultures. Does the rise in the number of young people, irrespective of the country's economic and social structure, mean a rise in radicalism; and conversely, does an aging population necessarily mean more conservatism? Though insurrectionary movements in Cuba, Vietnam, Angola, and elsewhere in the developing world appear to be essentially movements of young men, as were revolutionary movements in the past, cannot we also point to countries with large numbers of young people which have not experienced revolutionary upheavals? If so, one could argue that an increase in the number of young adults may be a necessary, but not sufficient, condition for revolutionary movements. However, one can readily see factors at work in many developing societies which would encourage an increasingly youthful population to be revolutionary.
>
> Insofar as many developing societies continue to remain age-ranked and older people continue to demand both respect and authority irrespective of their performance, young people are likely to become frustrated at the lack of opportunities made available to them within established institutions. If the young adult population increases more rapidly than job opportunities, then there will be a rapid increase in the number of unemployed or underemployed. Moreover, the movement of many young adults from villages, where traditional social controls continue to operate, to colleges and universities in the cities means that young adults are concentrated and, therefore, may be more able to organize as a cohesive political force. It does not follow, of course, that young people necessarily share a common political ideology or common political interest, but these factors may mean that a large youthful population is readily capable of being organized by various political groups.

The observation made by Moller, and the way Weiner takes it up and considers it, is simply one example of the way social scientists can contribute to our substantive understanding of the effects of rapid population growth. It will be clear moreover that their attempt at contributing to increased understanding depends on their specifying the problem. Rapid population growth in this example means growth in absolute numbers, and in the relative size of a particular age group and Weiner sets the hypothesis up not as a matter of simple cause and effect, but as one concerned with the conditions out of which revolutionary activity emerges; and here, as he makes clear, what appears particularly significant is the concurrence of a particular state of population with a series of other circumstances.

3.4 Conclusion

In this section we have considered two different sorts of issue: the first being the substantive question of what are the supposed political

---

[1] Weiner, M. (1969), *Political Demography: an Inquiry into the Political Consequences of Population Change*, National Academy of Sciences, pp.20–22.

effects of population growth. From the examples chosen it appears the question is a complex one and the sort of generalisations often made do not appear consistent with the evidence. The second issue we have taken up has been the role of the political scientist in this area. Here, as in the case of that of the sociologist discussed earlier in the unit, the emphasis has been on his actual and potential contribution to a greater understanding of the relationship between population growth and political activity, rather than to the solution of any of the practical problems such a relationship might produce.

TEST 4

"How I'd like to get married and get away from all this"

Figure 35.15

4 GENERAL CONCLUSION

This unit has been exploring two general questions. The first has been a substantive one concerned with the actual social and political implications of rapid population growth – the so-called population problem. Here the 'population' problem turns out to involve a huge range of untested assumptions and disputed interpretations. In pointing to these, emphasis has been placed here, as in previous sociological units, on the interrelated nature of society. Population factors are interrelated in complex ways with a whole range of other social and indeed political factors in society. Moreover there is great diversity in these patterns of interrelationships among societies, with the result that generalisations which may look convincing in the context of one society appear false in another. The complexity and diversity of actual interrelationships across the world is greater than much conventional wisdom would allow.

The second concern of this unit has been to indicate the particular contribution that sociologists and political scientists can make on this problem, and by extension say something about the value of social science. The character of the population problem and the relative newness of it as an area of empirical investigation in the social sciences has meant that the main emphasis in this unit has been on the contribution that can be made to understanding what is taken to be a problem; and within the realm of understanding, attention has been directed to the process of clarifying the problem, breaking it down and defining it in such a way that it can be tested against actual human situations. Some aspects of conventional wisdom have in addition been set against what data there is on the relationship and the processes of empirical enquiry illustrated with Weiner's article in the *Reader*. The state of enquiry on this aspect of society is less developed than in others and less can be said with confidence as a result about broad regularities in relationships. What is indicated in this unit about the approach of social scientists is that a degree of understanding is actually and potentially available greatly to assist those for whom population growth or the supposed effects of it are a problem which they are required to remedy.

The population explosion is a relatively recent phenomenon. Only thirty years ago Western opinion was more concerned with the problems posed by what was then thought to be incipient population decline. Since it is a new phenomenon, the empirical findings of social scientists are not only relatively few in number, but are at that stage of enquiry where the variety, the complexity of human experience, is more likely to emerge than the broad regularities.

TEST 5

ACKNOWLEDGEMENTS

Grateful acknowledgement is made to the following sources for material used in this unit:

Text

Asia Publishing House, for A. AIYAPPAN, *Social Revolution in a Kerala Village*; Clarendon Press, for H. K. BEAUCHAMP (trans. and ed.), *Hindu Manners, Customs and Ceremonies*; Doubleday & Co., for H. S. COMMAGER, 'Over Population and the New Nations', in F. OSBORNE (ed.), *Our Crowded Planet: Essays on the Pressures of Population* and J. ROBBINS, *Too Many Asians*; *Enquirer and News*, Battle Creek, Michigan, for editorial, 18 April 1965; National Academy of Sciences, for M. WEINER, *Political Demography: An Inquiry into the Political Consequences of Population Change*; National Research Council for, *The Growth of World Population*; Penguin Books Ltd., for A. ALLISON (ed.), *Population Control*; Population Reference Bureau for, *Population Bulletin*, December 1958; Prentice-Hall Inc., for H. F. DORN, 'World Population Growth' in P. M. HAUSER (ed.), *The Population Dilemma*; *The Times*, for article by D. WOOD, 8 March 1971; U.S. Senate Sub-Committee on Foreign Aid Expenditure of the Committee on Government Operations, *Population Crisis*, Vols 1 and 2A.

Illustrations

The *Daily Mirror* for Figs. 35.1–35.6 and 35.8–35.15; International Union for the Scientific Study of Population for Table 1 in Proceedings of the International Population Conference, 1962, Vol. IV; Penguin Books Ltd. for Fig. 35.7; Weidenfeld and Nicolson Ltd. for Table 2 in, E. A. WRIGLEY, *Population and History*.

BIBLIOGRAPHY

AIYAPPAN, A. (1965). *Social Revolution in a Kerala Village.* London, Asia Publishing House.

ALLISON, A. (ed.) (1970). *Population Control.* Harmondsworth, Penguin Books Ltd.

ANON (1961). 'The impact of uncontrolled birth on our democratic process'. *Humanist,* January-February.

ANSTEY, V. (1929). *The Economic Development of India.* London, Longmans.

BEAUCHAMP, H. K. (1924). *Hindu Manners, Customs and Ceremonies.* Oxford, Clarendon Press.

BENEDICT, B. (1970). 'Population regulation in primitive societies' in A. Allison (ed), *Population Control.* Harmondsworth, Penguin Books Ltd.

BERGER, P. L. (1966). *Invitation to Sociology.* Harmondsworth, Penguin Books Ltd.

BOSERUP, E. (1970). 'Population growth and food supplies' in A. Allison (ed), *Population Control.* Harmondsworth, Penguin Books Ltd.

BRASS, W. (1970). 'The growth of world population' in A. Allison (ed), *Population Control.* Harmondsworth, Penguin Books Ltd.

CHANDRASEKHAR, S. (1961). *Population and Parenthood in India,* 2nd edition. London, Allen and Unwin.

CHINOY, E. (1967). *Society.* New York, Random House. Open University edition.

COMMAGER, H. S. (1962). 'Overpopulation and the new nations' in Osborn, Fairfield (eds.), *Our Crowded Planet: Essays on the Pressures of Population.* New York, Doubleday.

COMMITTEE ON SCIENCE AND PUBLIC POLICY OF THE NATIONAL ACADEMY OF SCIENCES (1963). *The Growth of World Population.* National Research Council.

DAVIS, KINGSLEY (1967). 'Population policy: will current programmes succeed?, *Science,* 158, pp. 730–9. Reprinted in G. J. Demko, H. M. Rose and G. A. Schnell (eds.) (1970), *Population Geography: a Reader.* New York, McGraw-Hill.

DAVIS, KINGSLEY (1968). *The Population of India and Pakistan.* New York, Russell and Russell.

DAVIS, KINGSLEY and BLAKE, JUDITH (1956). 'Social structures and fertility: an analytic framework', *Economic Development and Social Change,* 4, 3.

DORN, H. F. (1963). 'World population growth' in P. M. Hauser (ed), *The Population Dilemma.* Englewood Cliffs, New Jersey, Prentice-Hall Inc.

EHRLICH, PAUL (1969). 'Eco-catastrophe!' *Ramparts,* September.

FREEDMAN, R. (1963). 'Norms for family size in underdeveloped areas' in *Proceedings of the Royal Society,* Series B, 159, 1963. Reprinted in the *Reader,* pp. 655—669.

HAUSER, PHILIP M. (1965). 'Demographic dimensions in world politics' in L. K. Ng, et al (eds.), *The Population Crisis*. Bloomington, Indiana, Indiana University Press.

HAWTHORN, G. (1970). *The Sociology of Fertility*. London, Collier-Macmillan.

HEER, D. M. (1968). *Society and Population*. Englewood Cliffs, New Jersey, Prentice-Hall Inc.

HUXLEY, JULIAN (1956). *Scientific American*, March.

INDIA PLANNING COMMISSION (1961). *Third Five Year Plan*. New Delhi.

KUMAR, KRISHAN (ed) (1971). *Revolution*. London, Weidenfeld and Nicolson.

LEWIS. O. (1958). *Village Life in Northern India*. University of Illinois Press.

MARSHALL, T. H. (ed) (1938). *The Population Problem: the Experts and the Public*. London, Allen and Unwin.

MOLLER, HERBERT (1968). 'Youth as a force in the modern world', *Journal of Comparative Studies in Society and History*, April, pp. 237–60.

MYINT, H. (1964). *The Economics of the Developing Countries*. London, Hutchinson University Library. Extract reprinted in the *Reader*, pp. 645–8.

MYRDAL, GUNNAR (1940). *Population: a Problem for Democracy*. Cambridge, Mass., Harvard University Press.

POPULATION REFERENCE BUREAU (1958). 'India: high cost of fertility', *Population Bulletin*. Washington, December.

ROBBINS, JOHN (1959). *Too Many Asians*. New York, Doubleday.

SCHNORE, L. F. (1961). 'Social problems in the underdeveloped areas: an ecological view', *Social Problems*, 8.

SEKHAR, CHANDRA A. (1971). 'Some aspects of the urbanisation of population in India', *Proceedings of the International Population Conference 1969*, vol. iv, pp. 2883–91. Liège, The International Union for the Scientific Study of Population.

SRINIVAS, M. N. (ed.) (1960). *India's Villages*, 2nd edition. Bombay, Asia Publishing House.

UNITED NATIONS (1970). *Demographic Yearbook 1969*. New York, United Nations.

UNITED STATES SENATE SUB-COMMITTEE ON FOREIGN AID EXPENDITURE OF THE COMMITTEE ON GOVERNMENT OPERATIONS. *Population Crisis*. 89th Congress, 1st session, Vols. 1 and 2.

WEINER, M. (1969). *Political Demography: an Inquiry into the Political Consequences of Population Change*. National Academy of Sciences.

WEINER, M. (1967). 'Urbanisation and Political Protest', the *Reader*, pp. 669–73. *Civilisation*, Vol. 17.

WOOD, DAVID (1971). *The Times*, 8 March 1971.

WRIGLEY, E. A. (1969). *Population and History*. London, Weidenfeld and Nicolson.

ZELINSKY, W. (1966). *A Prologue to Population Geography*. Englewood Cliffs, New Jersey, Prentice-Hall Inc.

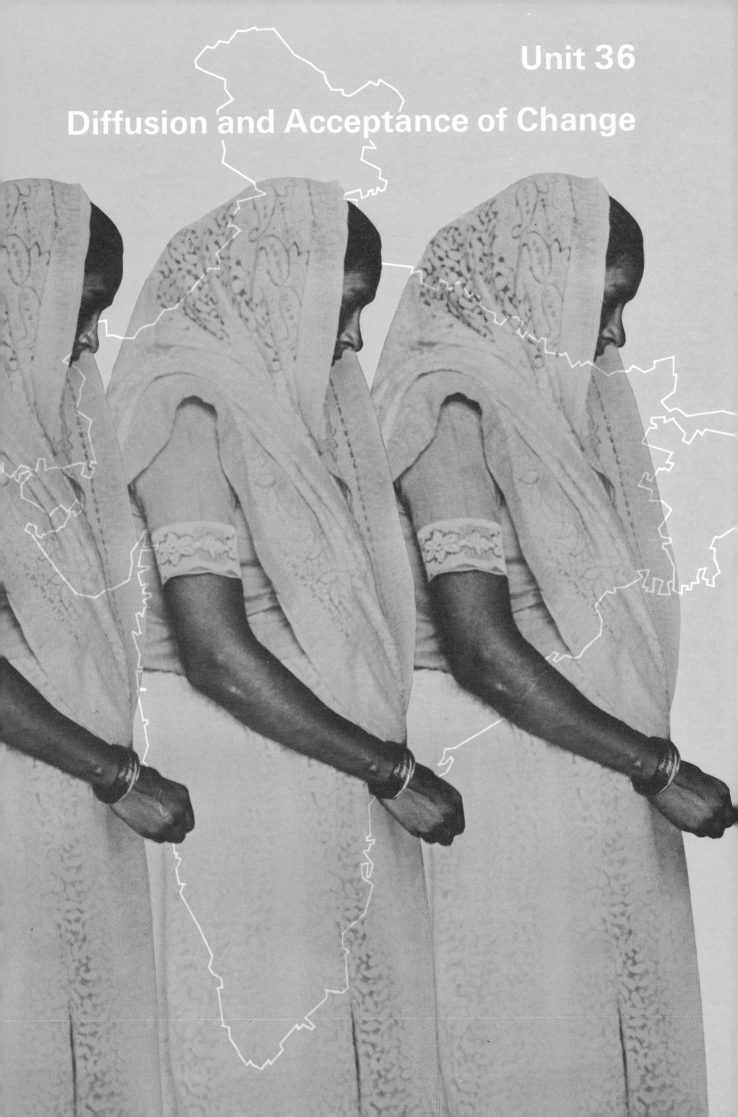

Unit 36
Diffusion and Acceptance of Change

CONTENTS UNIT 36

		PAGE
1	INTRODUCTION	143
2	ETHICAL PROBLEMS	144
3	STAGES IN THE PROCESS OF ADOPTING AN INNOVATION	146
4	SELECTIVE EXPOSURE AND THE CAPTIVE AUDIENCE	147
5	CATEGORIES OF INNOVATORS	148
6	SOCIETAL AND GROUP NORMS	148
7	SOCIAL INFLUENCE PROCESSES	150
	7.1 The Role of Information in the Process of Change	150
	7.2 Communicator Credibility	151
	7.3 Information and Influence	151
	7.4 Opinion Leaders, Innovators and the Mass Media	151
	7.5 Motivation Towards Change	154
8	PERSONALITY AND SOCIAL STRUCTURE	156
9	THE INDIAN EXPERIENCE	158
	9.1 Introduction	158
	9.2 The 1950s	158
	9.3 The 1960s	160
	9.4 Family Planning Education and the Mass Media	164
10	CONCLUSION	166
	BIBLIOGRAPHY	169
	ACKNOWLEDGEMENTS	170

ACKNOWLEDGEMENT

My sincere thanks are due to Dr. K. N. Kashyap, Medical Advisor to the Indian High Commissioner in London, and to the staff of the International Planned Parenthood Federation in London for information on Indian family planning policies and problems.

THE DIFFUSION AND ACCEPTANCE OF CHANGE

1 **INTRODUCTION**

The preceding units in this block of the course have explored the measurement of population change; regional variations in population pressures in India; the economic implications of rapid population increase; and finally the social and political problems arising from population growth. I think we can accept that there is fairly general agreement that population growth (caused by improvements in medicine and public health rather than an increase in procreation) is a serious world problem – in economic, ecological and social terms. If this problem is not to solve itself by mass starvation, wars or epidemics, and if we reject euthanasia as a means of keeping up the death rate, then we must find ways of reducing birth rates. But, though the means to do this exist, their adoption depends on voluntary acceptance and on an understanding of the need for birth control – in terms of the benefits accruing to an individual couple and their children and/or in terms of national or world considerations. This unit therefore investigates the problems associated with the diffusion and acceptance of social innovations.

The present unit deals with family planning in India. It is divided into two parts. In the first part we shall examine some of the very large body of research that has been done in the wider field of communications, attitude-change, motivation and the adoption of innovations. In the second part we shall look to the Indian experience and examine in what ways the principles derived from this wider field of study are being applied in India, so as to facilitate the introduction, acceptance and continued use of family planning measures. In this unit then we are firstly and mainly concerned with gaining an understanding of some aspects of *the social psychology of social change*; the Indian material serves as a case study. The unit, therefore, builds on some of the conceptualisations and material of previous psychology units (particularly Units 6, 8 and 31); it also links with the sociological discussion of social change in Unit 30.

The study of social change is most fruitfully approached from the perspectives of a number of social sciences; in particular, psychology and sociology, the principles of which are interwoven in this field. This point of view is also expressed in the reprint from the *International Encyclopaedia of the Social Sciences* of an article by Wilbert E. Moore on 'Social Change' which you received with Unit 30. Moore defines social change as:

> . . . the significant alteration of social structures (that is, of patterns of social action and interaction), including consequences and manifestations of such structures embodied in norms (rules of conduct), values, and cultural products and symbols.

We might extend this definition by stating that in the study of social change we are concerned with examining the possibilities of:

1 Changing the individual directly, through information (interpersonal or from the mass media), or through training in new skills and the offer of incentives for their adoption or practice.

2   Changing the individual through new group memberships or through changing the norms of existing groups.
3   Identifying the people (so-called opinion leaders) through whom to introduce and spread a particular innovation or information about the innovation.
4   Changing the 'social system' (new laws, credit systems, transport improvements, etc. etc.) to enable people to change 'pari passu' (or a little later!).
5   Influencing the growing generation along new lines in the family, kindergarten, schools or youth movements.

These points are linked with identifying what people's motives and expectations are with regard to a particular innovation and to present the innovation as something that meets these needs. For instance, in India, where children are highly valued, family planning must be presented as something positive, as something which is *for* children, not against them. How one might attempt to do this will be discussed later in this unit. In relation to the above points we must also study the *nature and characteristics of an innovation*. For instance, if a particular innovation can be adopted piecemeal and gradually, it is more readily accepted, but its fit or lack of fit with strongly held cultural values and existing needs and motivation is even more important.

The term 'innovation', of course, covers a great many different kinds of things.

Some innovations are completely new in the sense of being new discoveries for humanity in general, while others are the discovery by some communities of things already well-known to others. Some innovations relate to consumer goods, others to methods of production; still others may have no immediate practical application (e.g. discoveries in astronomy), yet may be profoundly disturbing to previously-held beliefs. Some innovations might have to be 'embodied' in specially built (and therefore expensive) equipment while others do not and can be adopted immediately. Some innovations are in themselves relatively small and unimportant, while others are large and revolutionary. Finally, some are capable of being adopted by individuals, others can only be implemented by organisations – e.g. business firms installing a new type of steel furnace – or by governments. I have already made the point that some changes initiated by, say, a government (and which I called 'social system' changes) facilitate innovation by individuals.

2   ETHICAL PROBLEMS

Perhaps it would be right, at the outset, to state that in studying why and how and when change takes place, and in using the understanding we thus gain to develop strategies to help the introduction of a specific change, we are facing not only complex *scientific* but also *ethical* problems. Social scientists are, however, not necessarily better qualified than anyone else to judge the moral and ethical implications involved in influencing other people. The only respect in which social scientists may be better qualified to judge the benefits of a particular change is in the training they have received (or should have received) of thinking in terms of the wider ramifications and implications of a proposed change. Thus, a social scientist acting as a 'change-agent' (a person who introduces a change) would at least consider whether the introduction of a particular change would have effects additional to those intended. Two examples may suffice at this stage. Introducing farmers in developing societies to more efficient methods of farming might be considered wholly beneficial. However, for instance, Jones (1966) has shown in relation to the Plateau Tonga of Zambia, that the adoption of such practices might lead to status incongruence, since in this society a *young* farmer is not supposed to be well-to-do. In terms of exchange theory his 'rewards' would outstrip his 'investments' and this would be psychologically uncomfortable. Hence, in fact, here as so often, a particular new farming practice was *learned* but not adopted except by those who (for various reasons in their past development and present situation), did not take their present 'membership group' as a valid psychological 'reference group'.[1] Another example of an 'improvement' which had unplanned consequences is quoted by Rogers (1962). He relates the case of an aboriginal tribe in Australia who were given steel axes (as gifts or in payment for work) by missionaries to replace their relatively ineffective stone axes. Previously, the stone axe was a symbol of masculinity and of respect for elders. The men owned the axes but women and children used them and borrowed them from fathers, husbands or uncles in accordance with their own customs. This tribe obtained the stone axe heads in exchange for spears through barter with local tribes at elaborate seasonal feasts. The steel axes, however, were distributed to men and women, young and old, and hence disrupted the tribe's status relationships and also led to the breakdown of their trading arrangements and rituals with neighbouring tribes. They were unable to adjust to the innovation though one cannot, of course, attribute their decline to just this one change.

It is perhaps interesting, in passing, to mention that research into mass media and communication effects started in the 1930s, because of the anxiety of social scientists at how mass media might be misused for propaganda purposes by European dictators. Since the Second World War, the emphasis in these studies has been on how one might structure the information situation, so as to ensure the acceptability of information relating to, say, a health campaign.

As this unit will illustrate, the 'wicked dictator' and the 'good campaigner' would appear to have an equally difficult task. You will already be alerted to the difficulty, but not the impossibility, of changing people from your reading of Unit 31, where, in Section 8, we discussed some deliberate attempts at changing people's values or ideologies. Although this unit is mainly concerned with exploring such scientific knowledge as we have about the processes of social change you ought to keep the moral and ethical issues in mind. *If one can change norms, who is to decide what they ought to be? Who is to prescribe aims and goals?* The social sciences themselves do not provide these value judgements, though individual social scientists may make them on the basis of their own values. In presenting an analysis of, say, the problems of introducing family planning into a community, a social scientist acts *qua* social scientist.

---

[1] A detailed discussion of these terms is included in Unit 31. Briefly, one can be a member of a group by virtue of one's physical presence in the group without thinking of the members of such a group as relevant persons with whom to compare oneself. Conversely, one can orientate one's behaviour towards the standards of a 'reference' group of which one is not in fact a (physical) member.

In actively helping to create a family planning campaign he has relinquished his neutrality and he should do so with due humility. He might quite easily find himself in a position similar to that of the physicist whose work is used to produce nuclear weapons. If the student feels that this is too shocking a parallel to imply he need only think of some of the horrifying uses to which the (neutral) knowledge of 'conditioning' (which we discussed in Unit 6) has been put in the so-called aversion treatment of alcoholics or sex perverts.

3 STAGES IN THE PROCESS OF ADOPTING AN INNOVATION

At this point in our discussion I should clarify the customary meaning of certain words used in the literature on innovation. The word diffusion (of new ideas or new practices) usually refers to the processes involved in spreading knowledge about an innovation and kindling interest in it among a given *population*. The words *adoption* or *acceptance*, however, refer to the psychological processes through which an *individual* passes, from first becoming aware of an innovation, to the point at which he finally adopts it. In this process of adoption (or rejection) a person usually passes through *conceptually distinct* stages or steps over a period of time. Rogers (1962) in reviewing research into the adoption of change in many different types of situations suggests that there are 5 stages:

(i) THE AWARENESS STAGE

The individual becomes aware of an innovation, possibly by chance. He hears a broadcast on family planning, he sees a neighbouring farmer use for the first time, say, contour ploughing. The individual at this stage is not yet motivated to seek further information. Whether or not he will do so may depend on his personality and attitudes, his need for the innovation and whether it fits in reasonably well with his present way of life or knowledge; it also depends on the extent to which similar changes are taking place in his social environment and on his relationships with the members of various groups and social networks of which he is a part. These same factors also influence how he progresses through the other stages in the diffusion process described here.

(ii) INTEREST STAGE

At this stage the individual becomes more psychologically involved in the innovation; he actively seeks information and he gains *knowledge* about it.

(iii) EVALUATION STAGE

At this stage the individual is assessing the innovation, its advantages and disadvantages, his fears and hopes.

(iv) TRIAL STAGE

At this stage the individual explores and experiments and adopts the innovation in a *limited* way to convince himself of the appropriateness of the new practice. Thus, a farmer may use a new type of seed grain in one of his fields but not in others. Some innovations, of course, cannot be adopted piecemeal – sterilisation as a method of birth control is for all practical purposes irreversible whilst other methods such as the use of the condom can be adopted on a trial basis. A person may therefore decide to practise some form of family planning and choose initially a method or device which lends itself to partial adoption.

(v) ADOPTION STAGE

At this point the individual decides to adopt the innovation and to continue to do so in future. An individual, of course, may *discontinue* using an innovation at a later stage just as he may reject it at any stage in the adoption process.

It is useful to keep in mind these stages in the adoption process since (as we shall see later in this unit), research has shown that the individual is receptive to different cues and to different sources of information (mass media or interpersonal sources), at these different stages. Hence, if one thinks in terms of developing a *strategy for change* (or indeed if one merely wants to understand why individuals adopt or reject particular innovations), these stages provide a useful conceptual framework.

4 SELECTIVE EXPOSURE AND THE CAPTIVE AUDIENCE

However, these descriptions of conceptually distinct stages in the adoption process and of characteristics of individuals at these various stages do not *explain* how and why the individual is changed and moves from one stage to the next. How is 'awareness' turned into active 'interest'? How does one move from 'interest' to 'evaluation'? In Units 29 and 30 it was repeatedly emphasised that no unitary or simple causes can be found as 'explanations' of change and I do not think that one can necessarily pinpoint the causes or even the mechanisms through which an individual proceeds from one stage to the next. Indeed, it would be easier to produce hypotheses as to why he should *not* proceed from one stage to the next. In Unit 8, p. 75 for instance, the student was alerted to the phenomena of 'selective exposure' or 'selective avoidance' (though these words were not in fact used). These concepts imply that people pay attention to information if it supports their present predilections, interests and knowledge and that they avoid 'disconfirming' and uncomfortable evidence.

This simplistic formulation is, in fact, not very consistently supported by empirical research as other variables are also involved. For instance, a high level of confidence in his knowledge or opinions, or his intellectual curiosity, or his conception of fairness, may move a person to expose himself to unpalatable information. However, these concepts are still useful in highlighting differences observed in the effectiveness of attempts to change opinions or attitudes in a laboratory setting as compared to a 'field' situation.

In the laboratory, the communicator is faced with a *captive audience*. Greater changes in opinions can be observed in response to 'persuasive messages' in these experimental situations than when the effects of educational or propaganda campaigns in the field are being assessed. Here, the individual is free to expose himself to the information or not as he chooses. 'Exposure' is, of course, not the same as accepting the validity of the message or changing one's opinion but it is a necessary first step. It should be noted, however, that the differences in the communication effects in laboratory and field settings arise also from the different kinds of issues used to assess attitude change in these two kinds of studies. (See Hovland, 1959.)

However, the concept of the captive audience is useful as a pointer towards practical strategies – thus, women in a maternity ward may be a receptive captive audience for information on birth control!

5 CATEGORIES OF INNOVATORS

Another useful set of *descriptive* terms relates to the fact that not all individuals in a society or group adopt an innovation at the same time. Rogers (1962) suggests a typology of adopters. He lists the following:

INNOVATORS

Their interests and social links usually lie outside their own local communities. They are adventurous and enterprising.

EARLY ADOPTERS

Their links and their social standing are within their own communities. They should be used by change-agents to speed the diffusion process.

EARLY MAJORITY

They follow with deliberation but rarely lead; they are an important link in the process of legitimising innovations.

LATE MAJORITY

They adopt new ideas after the average member of the group – out of economic necessity or in response to increasing social pressures.

LAGGARDS

They are the last to adopt. Their points of reference are traditional values. They may well adopt an innovation at a time when it has been superseded by a more recent innovation which the innovators are using.

6 SOCIETAL AND GROUP NORMS

In the following sections we will look at two major and *interacting* sets of factors which are always relevant to an understanding of processes of change – whether these occur spontaneously or are deliberately encouraged. These factors are:

1 Societal and group norms, and
2 Communication and influence processes.

These two sets of factors interact because information reaches an individual through a number of 'filters'. One set of filters is constituted by a person's attitudes and values which are very largely (as the student knows only too well by now!) the product of his early socialisation in a particular cultural setting. These attitudes and values, however, may be modified by a person's present group memberships and these social networks may be thought of as a second set of 'filters'. The important point to note here is that in complex societies groups with very different norms may exist. This may be illustrated by two studies from the United States. These studies were undertaken quite independently but both showed that a person's relationship with his reference groups (whether these are synonymous with his *local* membership groups or not) affect his readiness to innovate. One of these studies, conducted by Ryan and Gross (1943) was of the adoption of a new type of seed corn by *farmers* in two communities in Iowa. These farmers belonged to a traditionally minded group. The behaviour of *doctors*, in relation to the adoption of a new drug, studied by Menzel and Katz (1955) also reflected their group membership, but in this case they belonged to a professional group (in the same overall culture) whose outlook was orientated towards expecting continuing advances and changes in medical knowledge. Of particular importance, however, is an individual's relationship with his group. This may help to explain whether he will be a relatively early or late adopter. Farmers who had strong ties in their local community were relatively slow in adopting the new practice. Among the doctors the reverse was found to be true – the more frequently a doctor was named by his colleagues as a friend or discussion partner, the more likely he was to be an early adopter of the new drug. Homogeneity of opinions in primary groups has often been demonstrated and is variously due to like-minded people getting together or like-situated people developing a common outlook.

One might suggest that the doctors' group membership related to their innovativeness in two ways. Being integrated into a medical network opens channels of information not available to the less well integrated doctors and their group belongingness also acts as social support for their views and practices when facing the risks of innovation. Showing how relations to a membership or reference group affect rejection or adoption of an innovation is of course not the same thing as explaining *why* some people relate themselves to their groups and why others don't. This is partly a question of other models and other information being available and partly an individual personality characteristic. It is also linked with a person's education and past experience. The relevance of group membership can also be observed right through a lengthy adoption period. If the 'early adopters' in a particular situation are in some sense deviants, the 'early' and 'late majority' adopt when the innovation has been accepted – that is, they still conform but to a changed group norm. On the other hand, where the well-integrated group member adopts the new practice as fitting in with his and his group's values, the genuine outsider (the 'isolate' in Moreno's terminology, see Unit 31, p. 75) may never be affected. He does not relate to the group and he does not care about the group members' opinions of him. Thus, the doctors in the drug study all had contacts in the medical profession, but some had closer personal links than others and were therefore more quickly affected by new views and information than those who were relatively more loosely associated with their professional colleagues. By contrast, in the fictional example of *The Long Distance Runner* (Alan Sillitoe, 1959) the young delinquent is portrayed as a complete outsider who rejects the values of the prison governor and the social system he represents and he therefore remains unaffected and uninfluenced.

The *compatibility* of an innovation or new idea with present knowledge and personal, group and cultural norms has also to be considered. A new plough may be adopted in a tradition-minded village because it may represent a very small change: agricultural tools are already in use, the innovation is only a small step forward, is visible (and therefore becomes known) and its use does not require new and complex skills. To ask a devout Hindu to kill his mangy cows is suggesting a major innovation that goes counter to deeply-held religious views and, as we know, is not acceptable. However, there seem to be few strong religious or moral taboos against family planning in the Hindu religion, and several surveys have shown that a majority of Indian couples, even in remote villages, want smaller families. An innovation may appear compatible and be adopted and later be abandoned – an instance of this happened in a Mexican village (quoted in Rogers, 1962) where a 'better' type of seed grain giving bigger and more disease-resistant yields was adopted, but then its use was quickly discontinued when it was found difficult to make the traditional tortillas from it. Had the change-agents thought more fully of the implications of the innovation they could either have found another improved strain of seed, which could be ground in the traditional way, or they could have taught a new way of making tortillas. In some cases then the culture of a community almost totally bars some innovations (e.g. Moslems eating pork), while other innovations may seem incompatible but may become acceptable when other changes precede or accompany them.

7 SOCIAL INFLUENCE PROCESSES

7.1 The Role of Information in the Process of Change

Since very few people are original thinkers and inventors, new ideas and new practices are usually conveyed through information. How does new information reach us and what are the factors involved which make us decide (or without conscious decision, move us) to accept, adapt or reject new knowledge and new practices? Information in the form of news, advice, comment and so on can come to us from relatives, friends, workmates, salesmen, in other words, through *interpersonal channels*. Information, however, is increasingly reaching us from radio and television programmes, newspapers, leaflets, books, records, tapes, films, posters or indeed correspondence courses. In other words, the information comes to us from the *mass media*. I should perhaps state at the outset that the effect of a communication – whether from the mass media or from interpersonal contacts – depends on a number of interlocking factors. Ultimately, it depends on how the individual *perceives the meaning* of the information and hence how he interprets it and reacts to it. His perception depends on his present values and attitudes, his knowledge and his group memberships, all of which influence how he sees the communicator and his message. We have already explored this problem to some extent in Unit 31, where we were concerned with (mainly) *spontaneous interpersonal communication and interaction in groups* – I tried to assess then how far and under what conditions the individual modifies his behaviour and outlook as a result of voluntary or involuntary group membership.

Psychologists have, however, also paid particular attention to various aspects of 'persuasive communications', that is, *information which is intended to have a predetermined effect on the audience*. For instance, Hovland, Janis and Kelley (1953) have studied in laboratory experiments (with what I previously called 'captive audiences'), the role of individual predispositions, source credibility, the organisation of the arguments in the message, the extent of previous familiarity with the arguments or problems, the salience (importance) of group membership, the effectiveness of emotional appeals, the discrepancy between the position taken in the experimental message and the attitudinal position of the recipients of the message, and so on. All of these are important in understanding communication processes though we cannot discuss all of them here.

7.2 Communicator Credibility

Of particular importance, however, in real life as well as in laboratory studies, is the *credibility* which recipients of information attach to its source. This factor can be quite easily established in laboratory experiments. Hovland and his colleagues, for instance, determined for their experimental subjects first which newspapers they regarded as trustworthy sources of information and which they did not. The *same* message about a particular topic was then given to two groups of subjects, but attributed to a trustworthy source in the first group and linked to a less esteemed source for the second group. This kind of experiment repeatedly demonstrated that the impact of the same message varied according to the source from which it allegedly originated. This is a very important point to keep in mind when planning a strategy for the introduction of a particular change. Who, for instance, in what kind of group and situation, would be considered a reliable, authoritative and trustworthy source of family planning knowledge? The village midwife? The local headman? A famous doctor's voice on the radio? A series of newspaper articles? One's mother or one's friends? No definite answers can be given to these questions but the change-agent should always endeavour to find out who or what would be the most effective source of information to use for a particular campaign. However, as we shall see, *some* empirical generalisations are possible concerning the relative importance of the mass media and of personal influence at different stages of the adoption process.

7.3 Information and Influence

In this connection we should perhaps distinguish between the *transmission of information* and *influence*. Katz (1957) in the article reproduced in the *Reader* (pp. 674–84) shows that this differentiation relates to whether or not the mediator between the mass media and the general public merely acts as a relay or, whether in addition, he offers opinions selectively taken from the media or presented as his own views. The role of the 'transmitter' can be important in itself in keeping people in touch with events outside their personal experience. In isolated backward areas of the world, a person who travels regularly (a salesman or long-distance bus driver, for instance), or a literate person who reads the paper to others, or the owner of the only radio set[1] in a village, can fulfil this 'watchman' function, as Schramm (1964) calls it.

7.4 Opinion Leaders, Innovators and the Mass Media

In the article referred to, Katz discusses the concept of the *opinion*

---

[1] In 1967 there were only 7,579,000 radio and 6,000 television sets in India for a population of nearly 537 million (figures from Situation Report, Jan. 1970. *International Planned Parenthood Federation*). TV is limited to areas round a few leading cities but much larger groups than we are accustomed to in Britain view or listen to a set.

leader and shows that the opinion leader acts as a channel for new information *and* as a person who influences others. *An opinion leader is a person to whom others turn for advice* in situations where they face uncertainty. (By definition, the opinion leader does not seek *actively* to influence others.) He therefore plays an important part in the spread of new ideas and practices. The term 'opinion leader' was first used by Lazarsfeld and his colleagues (Lazarsfeld, Berelson and Gaudet, 1948) when they found, in studying changing voting intentions in the U.S.A. presidential elections of 1940, that their respondents were more influenced by personal relationships than by exposure to the mass media, and that certain people were consulted more often than others. As always in the discussion of a psychological relationship one must examine how two interacting entities perceive each other. For someone to become an opinion leader he must be *perceived* as a source of valid information and therefore the characteristics of the followers and the surrounding circumstances must also be studied. Lazarsfeld and the researchers who followed him (see Katz, 1957) found that opinion leaders were much like their followers in various demographic characteristics, aspirations and interests, but were more alert in seeking information from the mass media *and* from other people. The original hypothesis of the 'two-step flow of information' (from the mass media via the opinion leaders to followers) was later seen as insufficient, in that a chain of person-to-person influences could be traced before a decisive influence of a mass medium was encountered. It was also found that opinion leadership – like leadership in general – is very specific: someone influential in the field of fashion is not likely also to be influential in the field of political opinions, or as Emery and Oeser (1958) observed when studying the adoption of agricultural innovations by Australian farmers, those who were influential on agricultural matters were not opinion leaders on local community affairs. The phenomenon of opinion leadership is due to informal spontaneous relationships, so informal that to study the relationship and processes one has to define an opinion leader in some arbitrary way – e.g. as a person who is consulted by at least four people over a particular issue. On the other hand, a *change-agent* whose ordained task it is to influence others, normally holds a *formal position* but he, too, must carefully consider how he is perceived by his clients. He is often rejected, as being too unlike his clients, in himself and in his purposes. Where advocated changes are incompatible with cultural norms, one mental defence mechanism which is relatively easy to operate is a hostile perception of the change-agent; thus, a famous study of an innovation which failed to find acceptance showed that the village women in a Peruvian village called Los Molinos looked unfavourably on the health visitor and could reject her influence by referring to her as a 'dirt inspector' (Wellin, 1955). 'Superior' knowledge alone does not, therefore, lead to opinion leadership, and both the change-agent or the local innovator, though successfully demonstrating their *competence*, may be perceived as deviants rather than as models to be followed. Where the innovator has a strategic position in the community or an information network – like the innovating doctors in the drug study already referred to – they become influential opinion leaders. One way of ensuring that a change-agent, say an agricultural expert, has the necessary status and relationships in the community to which he is attached, is to choose a local man and train him in the new skills or ideas. But even this may fail, for the very fact of having had training may make him suspect.

It is interesting to see that in societies in the process of modernisation opinion leadership often shifts from the traditional holders of such positions, e.g. the chiefs or village elders, to young men who, being better educated or having travelled, are seen as being better able to help others in the achievement of their new goals. In such a society innovators and opinion leaders may be the same people or they may have similar characteristics – these frequently include literacy, cosmopolitanism (i.e. they have urban experience), use of and access to mass media and so on; on the other hand in a traditional society the innovator may have these characteristics *but he is not followed*. The impetus for his own innovativeness may be his marginal status in his local community which leads him to seek new knowledge or acceptance into new groups; thus the one shopkeeper in a village of farmers may find himself in this psychological position; the few housewives in Los Molinos, referred to earlier, who adopted the advocated practice of boiling their drinking water (to guard against water-borne infections) considered themselves, and were considered by the other villagers, as outsiders, since they had lived there for only a few years. Other 'converts' in this village were individuals of low status who sought new alliances. One practical lesson to be gained from this is that the important people, strategically placed, must be won first – the campaign to gain acceptance for a new measure is doomed once deviants and individuals of low status become the early adopters. Recognising this is an important step forward, but implementing it presents difficulties, since the regard in which people are held may evaporate when they themselves are seen as having changed – too much in advance of their fellows.

Opinion leadership is, of course, a matter of degree, and innovations or new ideas are rarely accepted without some modifications. To explore and experiment, to discuss and watch others, to adopt in a limited way, all allow one to convince oneself of the appropriateness of the new practice over a period of time. This process of gaining new cognitions, attitudes and practical skills can also be facilitated by group discussions under the non-authoritarian guidance of an expert who can help with factual information.[1] This, in a way, can be looked on as the spread of opinion leadership throughout a group and it is a very effective method of decision-making when the problem is within the authority and capabilities of the members of the group to solve. Often, of course, a proposed beneficial change requires knowledge, organisational skill and finance beyond the means of a local group and discussions are then valuable in creating a climate of opinion favourable to change. Innovations introduced or imposed from outside the particular community are then more likely to be accepted than resisted and the learning of the necessary new skills is more easily achieved in an atmosphere free from anxiety. *Group discussions may also be helpful in hitching the perception of a proposed change to a favourable attitude complex* (for example, 'it is good for the children') – a connection which might not have occurred to the individual in isolation. This is a very important point. Although it is the individual who has to change

---

[1] Group discussions and their place in decision-making and in the adoption of innovations were discussed in Unit 31 in Sections 5.1, 5.2 and 5.3 (pp. 68–69).

his attitudes and/or behaviour in, say, adopting family planning measures, his *willingness* to do so may depend on what others in his social environment think and do with regard to the same issue. It is easier for an individual to change when those around him also change – when in other words, new group norms can be seen to evolve.

It has been mentioned earlier that opinion leaders have been found to be more active than others in seeking information and opinions from various mass media and that the ultimate effect of such media as radio, television, newspapers, books and magazines operating *via* the opinion leaders is difficult to assess, but is probably substantial and cumulative. But the mass media may also affect the rest of the community directly.

7.5 **Motivation Towards Change**

For a change-agent (coming from within or from outside the community), or for a local innovator to make any impact, their potential clients or followers must have *the desire to change*. Such desires may arise directly from dissatisfaction with a group's economic or social position, or it may be generated by new information. I have already stated (p. 147), that we do not know exactly how an individual moves from 'awareness' to 'interest' in the process of adoption. I have also pointed out that the influence of a communication, or even of a sustained campaign, is very marginal in conditions of 'selective exposure'. Causation is therefore probably multiple and in part dependent on interpersonal influences. Nevertheless, many authors do consider that the mass media play an important part in these early stages. A great many studies, undertaken in different countries (see e.g. Lerner, 1958, Emery and Oeser, 1958, Rogers, 1962, Schramm, 1964), have provided strong *correlational* evidence of links between social change and three factors: *literacy*, exposure to *urban experiences* and to *mass media*. These three factors are seen as providing actual or symbolic new experiences – they widen people's horizons. Lerner, for instance, thinks of these factors as being instrumental in developing what he calls 'empathy', that is the individual's capacity of being able to look beyond his immediate circumstances and 'see himself in the role of another'. This in his view is the *psychological* key for a transition from a traditional to a modern society. Such an individual will be geared to change and ready for new ideas; he begins to look on the mass media as windows on the world and he develops new aspirations.

Schramm, in the book referred to, develops similar conceptualisations. He attributes three important functions to the mass media. Firstly, they act as 'watchman', reporting on events, near and far, and in so doing they widen horizons and raise expectations. Secondly, the media contribute to social decision processes, since they provide information necessary for a 'dialogue' on various issues and in so doing they may influence some attitudes and ways of behaving. They can also make new practices look legitimate and appropriate by making people familiar with them. Thirdly, the media have a teaching role, in fact, Schramm says they act as an 'educational multiplier' speeding the growth and spread of literacy and new skills.

I think two observations should be made here. Firstly, one should perhaps not make global statements about the role of the mass media. For the mass media to be influential they should reflect the social conditions of a particular society. When TV programmes are imported they may portray an alien way of life – for instance, Peyton Place and Coronation Street are shown in Cyprus. One wonders whether in these instances a realisable alternative is presented; presumably such programmes are viewed as entertainment only and the characters do not become models to be emulated.

Secondly, the suggested functions of the mass media referred to above should be thought of as extremely tentative; they possibly represent pious liberal hopes. Each point could probably be countered by evidence which would seem to suggest factors operating in opposite directions. One should in this context also examine critically the differential effects of various media. A person who can read can make his own selection and once having obtained the material can refer back to it. On the other hand, the person who depends on information from radio, cinema or TV has far less opportunity to make his own choice and judgements. To that extent he may be more susceptible to 'propaganda'.

I have stated that the evidence for a link between literacy, mass media exposure, urban experience and degree of *willingness* and *ability* to innovate is mostly correlational; in other words we cannot be certain that there is a casual connection and, if there is one, which factor is cause and which is effect. However, there is some evidence of the *intervening* role of the media between what might be termed *antecedent* and *consequent* conditions. Rogers (1965), for instance, found in his study of five Colombian villages that the 'antecedents' of 'functional' (bare) literacy and cosmopolitanism (trips to urban centres) correlated most with media use. The strongest 'consequents' of media use included greater empathy, political knowledge, educational aspirations and more innovativeness in home and farm work. Almost all the studies on opinion leaders show that their *competence*, in part at any rate, derives from their use of the mass media, both of media which *inform* (e.g. advertising) and media which *legitimise* decisions (e.g. professional journals).

For instance, the doctors in the study by Menzel and Katz (1955), referred to earlier, who were more influential, were more likely to read a large number of professional journals than doctors of lesser influence. They also attended out-of-town professional meetings and were in touch with other medical institutions and societies. Opinion leaders, then, relate their followers to important aspects and events in the 'outside' world. Their *influence*, however, as I stated, depends not only on competence but on their position in the group. Tannenbaum and Greenberg (1968) summarise Rogers' (1962) findings concerning the interaction of mass media and personal influence as follows:
(a) most individuals become aware of innovations from the mass media and then discuss them with peers as they evaluate the idea;
(b) the first step of the two-step flow should be characterised as a transfer of information, the second as a spread of influence;
(c) personal contacts are most influential at the stage of evaluating the new idea (a stage falling between initial awareness and eventual adoption or nonadoption), among those who adopt late (early adopters rely more on impersonal information or experts), and in ambiguous situations; and (d) opinion leaders rely more on mass media, or on impersonal, technical sources of information; opinion leaders inform and influence other opinion leaders.

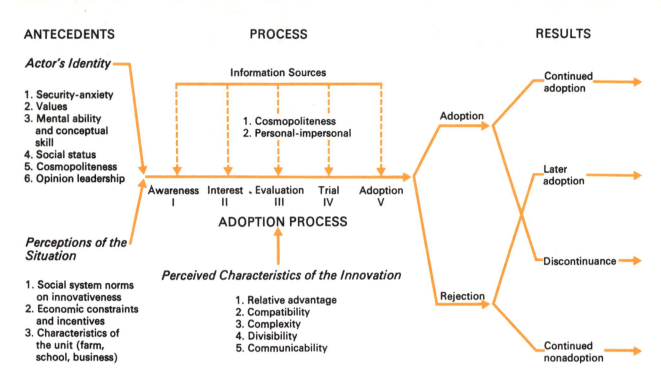

Source: E. M. Rogers: *Diffusion of Innovations*, 1962.

Figure 36.1 Model of the adoption of an innovation by an individual within a social system.

8 PERSONALITY AND SOCIAL STRUCTURE

In Section 6 of Unit 30 the question was raised whether the personality of individual men or women plays a part in bringing about social change. The scientific question to ask therefore is whether, among other factors affecting processes of change, personality can be thought of as an important mediating or intervening variable. You will recall the S – O – R formulation used in Unit 8 (p. 65). In our current context one could present this problem diagrammatically as follows:

In order to test this formulation one could, for instance, take a homogeneous sample of a hundred women, chosen for their similarity in ethnic background, age, marital history, number of live children, social class and education. We could then give such a group a personality test, and we might or might not find that the scores of those who are willing to innovate (e.g. to adopt birth control measures) are different from those not so willing.

The more homogeneous the group is, the more can the residual variability be accounted for in terms of personality traits or dimensions. However, this is an impractical approach in our present context since, in the sort of conditions in which a change-agent would be operating, he (a) cannot administer personality tests, and (b) he would, in any case, not be dealing with such preselected, homogeneous groups. In these real life situations individual personality differences are not of great importance since their contributions to the observed variability would be overlaid by other factors. It is interesting to note that personality has been variously defined in this context. Lerner (1958) to whom I have already made reference could be said to 'explain' social change in terms of the changing personality of the 'transitional' or 'modern' man in his typology. *But,* he expresses the characteristics of these people as arising from situational contexts – literacy, urban experience and media participation are seen to lead to empathy and willingness to change. The opportunities to change himself are not created by the individual's personality, they happen outside him though no doubt there are individual variations in responding to such opportunities. As was pointed out at the very beginning of this unit, innovation may involve changes in some structural aspect of the environment *and* in motivation, attitudes and skills. Which of these are antecedents and which are consequences cannot always be determined. *The locus of resistance to change, however, need not be looked for in the individual,* say in the farmer, who does not innovate, but in the situation of which he is part. Emery and Oeser (1958), for instance, who do regard 'personality' as the residual variable mediating between information and action categorise personality in demographic and sociological terms. They developed a typology of the farmer most ready to innovate which was based on the size of his farm, his past urban experience (for instance, during military service), use of mass media, his education and his present situational support (e.g. encouragement from his wife and help from his sons). All these can be seen to determine such of his psychological characteristics as his present knowledge, interests, attitudes and motivation which it would be more difficult (and offensive) to measure directly. The change-agent, in this case a District Agricultural Officer with limited time and resources, can maximise the usefulness of his efforts by pin-pointing, on these indices, the farmers most likely to be *willing* to expose themselves to new information and most *able* to adopt new techniques. In a community – like the Australian one studied by Emery and Oeser – geared to some extent to change, these innovating farmers will become opinion leaders and the change-agent's influence is diffused.

Changes in behaviour tend to be due to a number of simultaneous happenings. For instance, if a new road linking a hitherto isolated village to a town opens up a market for the local produce, it is at that point of time that farmers may become responsive to advice and help in setting up, for instance, a co-operative which owns transport and makes the marketing arrangements for its members. They may not have originated the construction of the road, which was decided on from outside (by the Government or other agency), but this change in their situation has further consequences and may move them towards changes which they themselves initiate. 'External' changes, of course, can be manipulated more readily than people, in order to create the context in which further change is possible. *The difficulty is to intervene on the social level in such a way that people and opportunities change at the same speed.*

Another question ought perhaps to be raised here. Lerner and Emery and Oeser emphasise that the adult personality changes in response to environmental and situational changes. However, other authors like McLelland (1961), whose doubtfully supported theory of achievement motivation was quoted in Unit 30, stress the importance of childhood socialisation. Hagen (1964) was troubled by the very slow transition he envisaged from 'authoritarian' static societies into 'innovating' creative ones, because the societies differed radically in the (modal) personalities they produced. I think that Hagen is too pessimistic since though a particular personality type may be dominant, probably the whole spectrum of personalities exists in any society. In changing economic or social circumstances different kinds of people are successful and their characteristics are unconsciously or consciously perpetuated by parents (and other socialising agents) who influence children along new lines.

Adjustments will not be perfect and they tend to happen with a time lag, but, nevertheless, the other authors I have referred to make one think that changes in outlook are more quickly achieved than Hagen supposed possible.

A whole course would be needed to examine properly the interaction of personality and social structure. The few comments made here merely serve to pose some of the questions and to link this unit to the discussion of social change in Unit 30.

9 THE INDIAN EXPERIENCE

9.1 Introduction

From previous units in this section of the course the student will know that there is, at any rate in certain areas of India, a population explosion and that this increase is due to a decrease in mortality rather than a rise in fertility. The Indian Government has since 1951 pursued a policy of fertility control and family planning and is spending considerable sums of money, both from its own resources and from foreign aid. In addition, private and international organisations are providing financial and other help. The birth-rate is at present (1971) estimated to be about 41 per 1,000 of the population and the Indian Government's stated aim is a reduction to 32 per 1,000 of the population by 1974 (though it is unlikely that this goal will be achieved) and eventually to 25 per 1,000 of the population.

We will now look at some of the policies and measures adopted in India and I will examine how far these may be considered to have utilised the kind of knowledge, on the diffusion and acceptance of change, discussed earlier in this unit.

9.2 The 1950s

I have already stated that in the Hindu religion – which is the majority religion – there are no taboos on family planning; against this must be set the fact that marriage in India is almost universal, that the marriage age is low, and that children are highly valued for economic and social reasons. By 1960, however, many studies indicated (Agarwala, 1962) that something like 70 per cent of married persons had favourable attitudes towards limiting and spacing the number of their children although only 10–20 per cent of women in rural areas had, at that time, any *knowledge* of contraceptive methods.

In view of the discrepancy between actual and desired size of family (see Table 1) and the stated willingness (see Table 2) to learn about birth control measures one might expect that information on birth control practices would be readily welcome and acted on. However, a number of early studies (Murty, 1968) showed that the *methods* advocated during the 1950s (rhythm method, coitus interruptus and foam tablets) were too unreliable and were not usually maintained though initially, at times, accepted. In other words,

TABLE 1

Ideal Size of Family as Reported in Selected Surveys in India

Study	Average ideal size	
Calcutta Study of Contraceptive Prevalence		
Higher profession and services (doctors, engineers, executives)	2·7	
Middle class – clerks, supervisors, retail traders	2·6	
Manual labor – skilled and unskilled	2·6	
Mysore Population Study	Wives	Husbands
Bangalore City, total	3·7	4·1
Muslim stratum	3·8	4·0
Scheduled caste stratum	3·7	4·3
Educated Hindu stratum	3·6	3·8
Less educated Hindu stratum	3·6	4·2
Rural plain (zone III)	4·7	4·6
Survey of fertility and mortality in Poona District (median)		
City sample		3·4
Non-city sample		4·0

Note: The above statistics should be compared with an actual average of between *6 and 7 children* ever born per married woman aged 45 in both rural and urban areas.

the *innovation* was unacceptable and impractical. Furthermore, it was found that the family planning clinics failed to attract sufficient clients. Many women who came to a clinic only did so once, and those who came belonged to the better educated section of the population. In other words, only a very small fraction of the 'target' population was effectively reached.

TABLE 2

Percentage of Persons Desirous of Learning More About Family Planning, or Favoring Family Planning

Study	Per cent
Ramanagaram – Lodi studies	
Ramanagaram	70·5
Lodi colony	75·8
Fertility survey, West Bengal[1] (Should an effort be made to limit the number of children? Proportion answering "Yes".	
Rural area	52
Towns	68
Calcutta City	67
Fertility survey of West Bengal, 1957. Would you approve use of contraceptives? Proportion answering "Yes".	
Rural areas	38
Towns	53
Calcutta City	61

Note:[1] Of those who did not answer "Yes", a very high proportion did not say "no", but merely lacked sufficient knowledge to express an opinion.

Source: Tables 1 and 2 (From 'Mass Communication and Motivation for Birth Control', *Proceedings of the Summer Workshop at the University of Chicago*. Edited by Donald J. Bogue. Published by Community and Family Study Center, University of Chicago, 1967).

9.3 The 1960s

Because of these findings, the family planning programme was reorganised in 1963 in order to translate the latent interest of individuals into action. The new approaches would appear to have utilised the insights gained from studies of the adoption of innovation. Family planning workers began to work through *local community leaders* or *opinion leaders* chosen from among interested 'early adopters' who were identified through certain scientific procedures and who were utilised for educational and service activities after being given adequate training. Information, advice, encouragement therefore came from people who already had a position of respect in a particular community and a central place in a network of communications. Where, for instance, a local midwife could be interested in family planning and be trained in advising on suitable methods, she would already be in touch with target groups – pregnant women and women who had recently had babies. Doctors in maternity hospitals were also trained in advising on family planning.

In the 1960s one favoured method of birth control was the condom. It is obviously important that when men had become interested in, and willing to use condoms, adequate supplies should be available. Local depot holders were therefore appointed and interestingly enough these were often the local postmen, again a set of persons with an extensive local knowledge and network of relationships.

In rural areas, knowledge was often spread with the help of mobile clinics which made regular visits to villages. These clinics attracted their audience initially by providing an entertaining *and* educational film show – a film show being a rare event in isolated rural areas. These shows would be followed by informal group discussions and advice to individual clients. From a psychological point of view one might say that such an approach should be more effective than merely advising individuals. Although it is an individual or a couple who have to change their ways, it is easier

Figure 36.2 Family Planning doctor distributes contraceptives on a tea estate in Assam.

for them to do so if they can see that other people also change their outlook and behaviour; or, as has been mentioned earlier, if new group norms can be seen to establish themselves. Group discussions with the aid of various 'change-agents' have been a widely used method. Another interesting way Indians have found of spreading family planning knowledge and acceptability is through the use of *satisfied acceptors*. Such people are obviously highly motivated, are part of the local community and hence not treated with suspicion, have local contacts and, with training, have proved to be very

Figure 36.3 Home-Visit by Family Planning worker demonstrating the Loop.

Figure 36.4 Visit by Mobile Family Planning Unit.

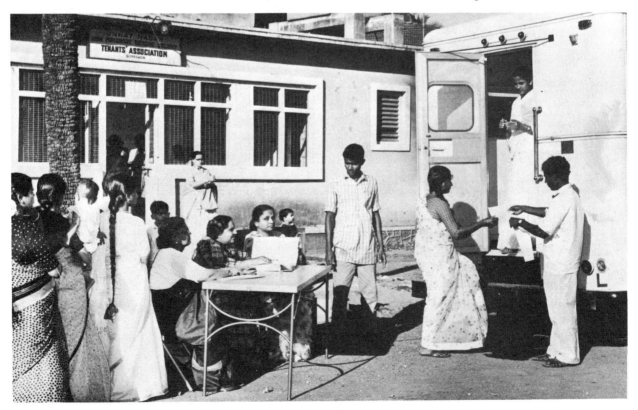

effective communicators. India (like some other countries) has gone further than this and has paid satisfied acceptors to motivate others to do likewise. These payments are chiefly offered[1] to promote long-lasting methods (the I.U.D. (intrauterine device) or male and female sterilisation); payments are made to the client, the 'canvasser' (who may be the local midwife, a friend or relative, possibly satisfied acceptors themselves) and the clinic doctor. The advantage of such virtually permanent or long-lasting methods is, of course, their relative cheapness, and the fact that their effects do not depend on *maintaining motivation* towards family planning in the acceptor. The *advantages* of using 'canvassers' or satisfied clients (paid on a piecework basis to maintain *their* motivation), are that such people have local roots and connections, are close to the target population in terms of social distance, can reach 'disadvantaged' segments of the community who are probably least inclined to visit a clinic and who are not usually exposed to education via the mass media. The *disadvantages* of this approach are that the

canvassers are 'entrepreneurs', motivated by pecuniary incentive rather than a concern for family welfare; that they sometimes bring along for sterilisation operations, clients for whom the service is not intended such as bachelors, men over age, or fathers with less than three living children, or that they neglect to obtain the consent of the wife. Nevertheless, this system has proved so effective that it is being maintained in spite of the disadvantages mentioned.

Figure 36.5 These men are meeting with the Family Planning workers after seeing a film at a mobile clinic which is visiting their village. (From the film: 'Years of Promise').

[1] 'Incentive Payments in Family Planning Programmes, Working Paper No. 4'. *International Planned Parenthood Federation*, London.

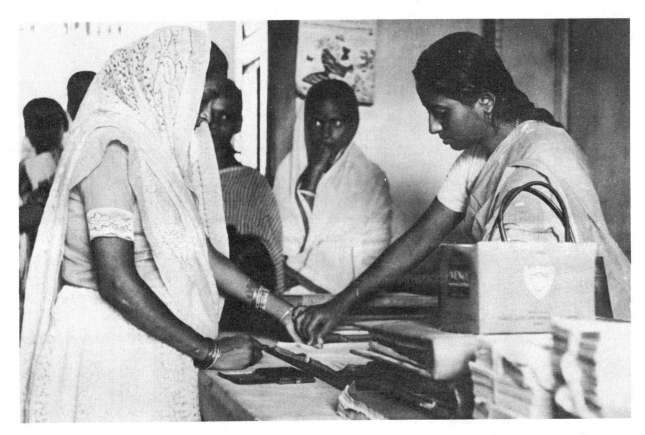

Figure 36.6 Women registering at a Family Planning Centre. The woman registering is illiterate (she signs with a thumbprint). Initially, the family planning campaigns reached the more educated section of the population but are now making a wider impact.

Studies of family planning campaigns in India show that one of the chief problems encountered concerns the maintenance of motivation and continuance of the use of various methods. Male and female sterilisation and, to some extent, the insertion of an intra-uterine contraceptive device overcome these problems and are at present the preferred methods of family planning in India. Official Indian estimates suggest that 7.5 million male and female sterilisation operations have been carried out up to the end of 1970. The estimated number of I.U.D. insertions at that point of time was 3.4 million. More conventional contraceptive users are estimated to number 1.5 million people (1969/70), 90 per cent of whom use condoms.[1] Though the figures for sterilisations and I.U.D. insertions are large by European standards, it must be borne in mind that these and other methods of birth control probably only reach at present something like ten per cent of the Indian population in the reproductive age groups.

We have earlier stated that clinics, when set up without the active participation of the community and its leaders, tended to be underused. Progress was made when, after 1965, family planning became 'respectable' by being made an integral part of medical and public health services and especially of mother and child health programmes. Infant mortality has been lowered and child health has been improved. This in itself makes family planning more attractive – no longer does a couple need to have many children to be certain that some will survive. Another important consequence is that in this way target groups can be more readily reached. As mothers take their children to clinics – for advice, free vitamins and so on –

[1] These figures have been supplied by Dr. K. N. Kashyap, Medical Advisor to the Indian High Commissioner in London.

family planning can also be discussed. Maternity hospitals or midwives working in the community are also, of course, in touch with the very people who might be receptive to family planning advice.

9.4 Family Planning Education and the Mass Media

From our general knowledge of the effects and the effectiveness of the mass media in relation to the adoption of innovations (discussed in Section 7), we would not expect the mass media to have an immediate and direct impact. We have seen that the mass media are likely to be effective in two ways: they can help in the early stages in creating *awareness* and in the crucial adoption stages they are effective *via* the face-to-face communicators who make more extensive use of the mass media than the followers. They may also play a part in *maintaining motivation* in the 'post-acceptance' stage. It would, therefore, appear that *different* mass media might be effective at different stages and with different people. Posters, for instance, have been widely used in India to create awareness and

stimulate interest in family planning and care has been taken to produce slogans which are *specific* rather than vague. One of the most widely used posters shows four faces (parents and two children) and the slogan 'Two or three children – stop'.

Other slogans are: 'A small family is a happy family',

'Three or two – that will do',

'Next child not now, after three, Never'.

The second slogan ('A small family is a happy family) stresses that limiting the size of the family does something positive for children.

Figure 36.7 A billboard on the street with the government of India's family planning slogan: 'A Small Family is a Happy Family'.

Figure 36.8 Family Planning Clinic. The couple (she aged 40 and he aged 45) have four children and are seeking family planning advice.

This is a very important tactic since in a society where children are greatly valued, family planning must be portrayed as something that is *for* children, not against them. To show that fewer children mean a better family life, better education and standards of living for the children is, therefore, important. The main aim of family planning education should be to help people, see how their values of love for family and children can be satisfied by having *fewer* children. In this connection we have already mentioned, for instance, that family planning advice can obtain a positive image by being provided in conjunction with other desirable services at child and maternity welfare clinics.

The poster overleaf shows the inverted red triangle which India has adopted as its symbol of family planning. It appears on all posters, outside family planning clinics, on contraceptive products and so on. It is probably a very effective psychological device: it is purely symbolic and therefore it has only one meaning – Family Planning. It is simple, visible, striking and it can be reproduced everywhere. It is the trademark of family planning in India.

Other mass media (such as pamphlets, films, newspaper articles, talks on the radio) are widely used and they are probably most effective when used *in conjunction* with interpersonal communications from change-agents or community leaders and as a basis for group discussions. Unlike posters and slogans, these media allow for detailed discussions of the 'why' and 'how' of family planning, they can deal with common queries and doubts and, of particular importance, they support, encourage and inform the community and opinion leaders.

A great variety of more traditional channels of information are also used in India, for instance, exhibitions, travelling puppet shows, song and dance groups.

Most major changes are easier to accomplish not by changing existing attitudes (nor even by showing new ways of satisfying these

Figure 36.9 The ubiquitous red triangle, symbol of India's family planning programme.

attitudes), but by influencing the growing generation to have different values. Efforts are, therefore, made in India to include the growing generation in the target groups for family planning education. School children can be 'sensitised' to the idea of the two-child family as 'normal' and beneficial, without necessarily mentioning any techniques of birth control at that stage. How far such approaches are likely to be effective is not as yet known. The ideas presented at school may be reinforced or contradicted at home and by the child's other contacts.

10 CONCLUSION

India has had an official policy of population control since 1951. In the early years, experiments with the safe period or rhythm method of birth control turned out to be relatively ineffective and unacceptable. Since the 1960s a much more vigorous campaign, based on more effective methods of birth control and more effective methods of mobilising awareness, interest and motivation has been in progress. What have been the results of these efforts? This is a most difficult question about which to say anything conclusive. Indian government statistics show no decline in the birth rate which, since 1960, seems to hover at the 41 per thousand mark. Such a figure, in the nature of things in a country like India, cannot be entirely accurate, and to this must be added the difficulties of interpreting the crude birth rate figures – a problem which is discussed in the television programme associated with Unit 32. A point to note is that fertility might well have gone up, in response to the slightly better standards of living and improved health and medical conditions in the country. But assuming it has remained steady, how far can this be attributed to the effects of the Indian policies for family planning? Again, one cannot be certain about this. It is obvious that where (for all practical purposes), permanent methods such as male and female sterilisation have been used, an estimate can be made of the number of births prevented (if the age groups of the acceptors are known). Again, knowledge of the percentage of couples in the fertile age-range who have begun to use other effective methods (I.U.D. or condom) and who can be motivated to *continue* contraception can lead one to estimate the likely number of births which have been or will be prevented. Such calculations, of course, leave out all those who do not practise birth control. Estimates again vary somewhat strikingly but it would appear that at present only about ten per cent of couples in the fertile age groups adopt a method of family planning. The effectiveness of any family planning campaign can only be assessed in the long term and its success depends very largely on how far it can create a *changed climate of opinion* and changed attitudes to what is considered a normal and acceptable family size. Of course, knowledge of birth control methods, availability of supplies, incentives to adopt permanent measures are important – but even without these people right through history have managed to limit their families, *when they were so inclined*.[1] Certain forms of birth control and abortion have probably been practised in all societies from time to time (see, e.g. Wrigley, 1966, concerning eighteenth-century England). However, *social norms and customs* (such as age at marriage, incidence of separation, divorce and remarriage, post partum sexual abstinence, abstinence during certain seasons (e.g. Lent) or ceremonies, celibacy and voluntary sexual abstention for economic or other reasons affect fertility significantly.

As we have seen Indian Family Planning campaigns are directed not only towards individuals but towards creating new social norms concerning family size and I have pointed out that this is a valuable strategy, since it is easier for people to change when others around them can also be seen to change. This is of necessity a slow process even where, as has been mentioned, there appears to be a

---

[1] Similarly, it is very difficult to encourage families to have *more* children than they want – 'pro-natalist' policies in pre-war France, Italy and Germany had very little impact. The political problems arising from a deliberate attempt to use 'societal controls over motivation' can be imagined if one looks at the list of measures suggested by Davis (1967). These include the charging of substantial fees for a marriage; a tax *on* children; the abortion of all illegitimate conceptions; higher tax rates for married than for single people; reductions in maternity and family allowances; the favouring of single people and childless couples in the allocation of housing; equal pay and educational facilities for women, so they may develop interests that will reduce the attractions of home and family.

latent desire to limit families though to 3–4 children rather than the advocated 2–3. It is impossible to judge from published data how far social norms are beginning to change (particularly in those areas where birth rates are rather high – Unit 33 discusses the great regional variations in the Indian birth rate). What one can say is that the Indian family planning campaigns do use the knowledge and insights gathered by social scientists concerning the diffusion and acceptance of change. Once social norms begin to change – *whether in response to campaigns or because of changing economic and social conditions* – the movement is likely to gain momentum. In Roger's terminology quoted on p. 148 the 'late majority' will begin to succeed 'the early majority'.

An interesting point is made by W. D. Borrie (1970). He says (p. 272): 'the prevention of births, even on a modest scale, can change the structure of a population quite markedly in favour of a higher level of net investment, for initially, and for a period of at least twenty-five years it reduces the burden of dependency without reducing the labour force, and so enhances the capacity of the economy both to increase its net investment and to use investment in more productive ways. It means, for example, less investment in schools and housing and frees more for investments that will increase both rural and industrial output.'

The implication of this quotation is that the short-term effects of family planning policies have beneficial short-term *and* long-term *economic* effects. It is unlikely that a country like India would wish, or could live up to the precept of diverting investment from, say, schools to industry in order to increase her economic potential, since her eventual standard of living would appear to depend on increasing both education and training opportunities *and* industrial development.

Borrie, however, supports the contention that birth control campaigns and techniques may aid economic changes which then in turn may produce long-term economic and social changes which in their turn lead to smaller families on the pattern of industrialised societies.

This seems a sensible position to take where some writers pin their faith and hopes on family planning campaigns and others completely deny their impact on fertility (the reduction in which is seen only as a result of economic and social changes). As W. D. Borrie says (p. 276), in the book already referred to: 'knowledge is much too imprecise yet to permit prediction of the effectiveness of the population policies now being implemented in developing countries, and as some of the countries with vigorous family planning programmes in which the birth rate has fallen are also those which have also clearly undergone major social and economic changes, the isolation of the precise influence of each of the many variables involved is an extremely difficult task'.

It may be momentarily disheartening for the student to end his first year course in the social sciences with this quotation. However, I think it is an appropriate quotation on which to end not only this unit but the course as a whole. The isolation of the precise influence of each of the many variables involved in any social situation or form of behaviour *is* an extremely difficult task and new scientific insights and knowledge can only be gained slowly and by rigorously conducted research. For those interested in this, the study of the social sciences is an intellectually exciting and rewarding pursuit.

BIBLIOGRAPHY

AGARWALA, S. N. (1962). 'Attitude Towards Family Planning in India', *Institute of Economic Growth, Occasional Paper No. 5*. Delhi.

BORRIE, W. D. (1970). *The Growth and Control of World Population.* London, Weidenfeld and Nicolson.

DAVID, K. (1967). 'Population policy: will current programmes succeed', *Science*, 158, pp. 730–9. Reprinted in G. J. Demko, H. M. Rose, and G. A. Schnell (1970), *Population Geography: a Reader*, New York, McGraw-Hill.

EMERY, F. E., and OESER, O. A. (1958). *Information, Decision and Action.* New York, Cambridge University Press.

HAGEN, E. E. (1964). *On the Theory of Social Change.* London, Tavistock Publications.

HOVLAND, C. I., JANIS, J. L., and KELLEY, H. H. (1953). *Communication and Persuasion.* New Haven, Connecticut, Yale University Press.

HOVLAND, C. I. (1959). 'Reconciling Conflicting Results Derived from Experimental and Survey Studies of Attitude Change', *The American Psychologist*, Vol. 14, pp. 8–17. Reprinted in M. Jahoda and N. Warren (eds.), (1966). *Attitudes, Selected Readings.* Harmondsworth, Penguin Education.

JONES, A. D. (1966). 'Change Agent and Client', in Brandt (ed.), *Communications Between Developed and Underdeveloped Nations.* Berlin, Institut für Entwicklungspolitik.

KATZ, E. (1957). 'The Two-Step Flow of Communication', *Public Opinion Quarterly*, Vol. 21, pp. 61–8. Reprinted in *Understanding Society*. London, Open University Press/Macmillan (1970).

LAZARSFELD, P. F., BERELSON, E., and GAUDET, H. (1948). *The People's Choice.* New York, Columbia University Press.

LERNER, D. (1958). *The Passing of Traditional Society.* Glencoe, Illinois, Free Press.

MCLELLAND, D. C. (1961). *The Achieving Society.* Princeton, Van Nostrand.

MENZEL, H., and KATZ, E. (1955). 'Social Relations and Innovation in the Medical Press', *Public Opinion Quarterly*, Vol. 19.

MURTY, D. V. R. (1968). 'Studies in Family Planning Communications in India', in *Asian Population Studies Series No. 3. Report of the Working Group on Communications Aspects of Family Planning Programmes and Selected Papers.* Bangkok, United Nations.

ROGERS, E. M. (1962). *Diffusion of Innovations.* New York, The Free Press.

ROGERS, E. M. (1965). 'Mass Media Exposure and Modernisation among Colombian Peasants', *Public Opinion Quarterly*, 29, pp. 614–25.

RYAN, B., and GROSS, N. C. (1943). 'The Diffusion of Hybrid Seed Corn in Two Iowa Communities', *Rural Society*, **8**, pp. 15–24.

SCHRAMM, W. (1964). *Mass Media and National Development.* California, Stanford University Press.

SILLITOE, A. (1959). *The Loneliness of The Long Distance Runner.* London, W. H. Allen.

TANNENBAUM, P. H., and GREENBERG, B. S. (1968). 'Mass Communication', *Annual Review of Psychology*, Vol. 19, pp. 351–86.

WELLIN, E. (1955). 'Water Boiling in a Peruvian Town', in B. D. Paul (ed.), *Health, Culture and Community*. New York, Russell Sage Foundation.

WRIGLEY, E. A. (1966). 'Family Limitation in Pre-Industrial England', in M. Drake (ed.) (1969), *Population in Industrialisation*. London, Methuen & Co.

ACKNOWLEDGEMENTS

Grateful acknowledgement is made to the following sources for material used in this unit:

Text

Annual Reviews Inc. for P. H. TANNENBAUM and B. S. GREENBERG, 'Mass Communication', in *Annual Review of Psychology*, Vol. 19, pp. 351–86; Macmillan & Co. for W. E. MOORE in *International Encyclopaedia of Social Sciences*; Weidenfeld and Nicolson for W. D. BORRIE, *The Growth and Control of World Population*.

Illustrations

Collier-Macmillan for Fig. 36.1, in E. M. ROGERS, *Diffusion of Innovations*; International Planned Parenthood Federation for Figs. 36.2, 36.3, 36.4, 36.5, 36.6; National Christian Council of India for Fig. 36.7; Oxfam for Fig. 36.8; University of Chicago Press for Tables 1 and 2, in D. J. BOGUE, *Proceedings of the Summer Workshop at the University of Chicago*.

Notes

Notes

Notes

Notes

Notes

Notes

Notes

Notes

Notes

UNDERSTANDING SOCIETY UNITS

1 WHY PEOPLE LIVE IN SOCIETIES

1. The Fundamentals of Human Nature
2. Men and Government
3. The Economic Basis of Society
4. Societies and Environments
5. Man as a Social Animal

2 HOW PEOPLE LIVE IN SOCIETIES

Socialisation

6. Child Socialisation
7. Personality Development
8. Attitudes and Prejudice
9. The Family and its Functions

Economy and Society

10. Economic Wants
11. Production and Supply
12. Markets and Prices
13. The Sociology of Economic Behaviour

Money, Wealth and Class

14. The Workings of the Economy
15. Money
16. Distribution of Incomes
17. Social Stratification
18. The Psychology of Social Class

Spatial Aspects of Society

19. Rural Land Use
20. Location of Industry
21. Zoning within Cities
22. The Size and Spacing of Settlements
23. Approaches to Political Geography

Government and Politics

24. The Formal Structure of Government
25. Informal Political Institutions
26. Government and Politics without the State
27. (1) Political Culture and (2) Politics and Political Systems
28. Politics in Groups

Stability Change and Conflict

29. Stability and Function in Society
30. Social Change in Society
31. Stability and Change in Social Groups

3 WHAT KIND OF PROBLEMS PEOPLE FACE IN SOCIETIES

The Population Explosion – an Interdisciplinary Approach

32. The Demographer and his World
33. Demographic Regions of the Indian Subcontinent
34. Population and Economic Growth
35. Population Growth and Social and Political Systems
36. Diffusion and Acceptance of Change